Global Standards and Publications

EDITION 2018/2019

Colophon

Title:	Global Standards and Publications
	Edition 2018/2019
Publication of:	Van Haren Publishing, www.vanharen.net
ISBN Hard copy:	978 94 018 0223 9
ISBN eBook:	978 94 018 0224 6
Print:	First edition, first impression, October 2017
Layout and design:	Coco Bookmedia, Amersfoort – NL
Copyright:	© Van Haren Publishing 2017

TRADEMARK NOTICES
ArchiMate®, IT4IT® and TOGAF® are registered trademarks of The Open Group.
ASL® and BiSL® are registered trademarks of ASL BiSL Foundation.
COBIT® is a registered trademark of the Information Systems Audit and Control Association (ISACA) / IT Governance Institute (ITGI).
ITIL® is a registered trademark of AXELOS.
M_o_R® is a registered trademark of AXELOS.
MoP™ is a registered trademark of AXELOS.
MSP® is a registered trademark of AXELOS.
P3O® is a registered trademark of AXELOS.
PRINCE2® is a registered trademark of AXELOS.
PMBOK® Guide is a registered trademark of the Project Management Institute (PMI).
SqEME® is a registered trademark of Stichting SqEME.

For any further enquiries about Van Haren Publishing, please send an e-mail to: info@vanharen.net

Dear readers,

You and we are well aware that we live in a Volatile, Uncertain, Complex, and Ambiguous (VUCA) environment. As a result, more and more professionals choose to apply agile approaches, but also many of them agree that there is still a need for standardization and collecting and applying best practices. In the first place because this helps communication with other professionals, referring to globally accepted terminology. And also, because it helps to apply a high-level approach for professional discussion.

Van Haren Publishing publishes easy to access publications on Best Practices that are developed by professionals and quality-reviewed by many other experts. This provides you with information summarizing years of experience by the best in the profession. It is an honor for us to collaborate with knowledge partners like ASLBiSL Foundation, IACCM, IPMA, ITSMF, ITWNET, IVI and The Open Group, to support their Best Practices and standards.

Not only do we publish books on Best Practices, we also actively and independently promote the standards and frameworks via many partners that carry our web shop. Since 2017 we offer a portfolio of Courseware products to support training organizations with their training courses on exams that are based on these best practice and standards.

The application of these best practices and standards is not more than a tool that enables professionals to get to better results. We understand that this is mainly about knowledge and skills. We also realize that the people factor is more important, since without people all these things don't evolve at all. Partly we also address this area through our publications that are based on competence, but we admit that we only cover a small area of this in the products we provide on this.

Anyway, we do our best to play a part in sharing the knowledge and skills from Best Practice and standards with our customers. The rest should come from you.

Kind regards,
The publishing team of Van Haren Publishing

Contents

IT & IT Management

Project Management

Enterprise Architecture

Business Management

IT & IT management

Agile

1 Title/current version

Agile

2 The basics

Originating from the world of IT where the concept of Agile refers to a set of software development methods based on iterative and incremental development, where requirements and solutions evolve through collaboration between self-organizing, cross-functional teams. Nowadays, the principles of the Agile approach are also used in other domains, for example design & engineering, product development, manufacturing, etc.

3 Summary

Incremental software development methods have been traced back to 1957. 'Lightweight' software development methods evolved in the mid-1990s as a reaction against 'heavyweight' methods, which were characterized by their critics as a heavily regulated, regimented, micromanaged, waterfall model of development. Supporters of lightweight methods (and now Agile methods) contend that they are a return to earlier practices in software development.

Early implementations of lightweight methods include Scrum (1993), Crystal Clear, Extreme Programming (XP, 1996), Adaptive Software Development, Feature Driven Development, DSDM (1995, called DSDM-Atern since 2008), and the Rational Unified Process (RUP, 1998). These are now typically referred to as Agile methods, after the Agile Manifesto.

The Agile Manifesto was written in February 2001, at a summit of independent-minded practitioners of several programming methods.

Manifesto for Agile Software Development

We are uncovering better ways of developing
software by doing it and helping others do it.
Through this work we have come to value:

Individuals and interactions over processes and tools
Working software over comprehensive documentation
Customer collaboration over contract negotiation
Responding to change over following a plan

That is, while there is value in the items on
the right, we value the items on the left more.

Source: agilemanifesto.org/

The Agile Manifesto has twelve underlying principles:

1. Customer satisfaction by rapid delivery of useful software
2. Welcome changing requirements, even late in development
3. Working software is delivered frequently (weeks rather than months)
4. Working software is the principal measure of progress
5. Sustainable development, able to maintain a constant pace
6. Close, daily co-operation between business people and developers
7. Face-to-face conversation is the best form of communication (co-location)
8. Projects are built around motivated individuals, who should be trusted
9. Continuous attention to technical excellence and good design

10. Simplicity
11. Self-organizing teams
12. Regular adaptation to changing circumstances

Agile methods break tasks into small increments with minimal planning and do not directly involve long-term planning. Iterations are short time frames. Team composition in an Agile project is usually cross-functional and self-organizing and team size is usually small (5-9 people). The Agile method encourages stakeholders to prioritize "their requirements on the basis of business value".

The Agile approach is supported by the Agile Alliance, a not-for-profit organization that wants to see Agile projects start and help Agile teams perform. It is funded by individual memberships, corporate memberships, and by the proceeds from the Agile conferences. It is not a certification body and does not endorse any certification programmes.

4 Target audience

Anyone involved in an Agile development project team; including analysts, architects, developers, engineers, testers and business customer/users; anyone supporting or managing an Agile project team who requires a detailed understanding of the practices and benefits of Agile development.

5 Scope and constraints

Applicable to development environments. Improved quality; higher productivity; positive effect on business satisfaction.

Constraints:
- Works less well in distributed development efforts where teams are not located together
- Acceptance: forcing an Agile process on a development team that is unfamiliar with the approach
- Exceptions: mission-critical systems where failure is not an option at any cost (e.g. software for surgical procedures)

6 Relevant website

www.agilemanifesto.org

Amsterdam Information management Model (AIM)

1 Title/current version

The Amsterdam model for Information Management: A Generic
Framework for Information Management

2 The basics

The Amsterdam Information management Model (AIM)
provides a mapping of the relationships between organization
and information.

3 Summary

AIM was developed at the University of Amsterdam (paper:
Abcouwer, A.W., Maes, R. Truijens, J. (1997), 'Contouren voor
een generiek model voor informatie-management', Tijdschrift
Informatie en Management). It can be used as a tool for positioning
and interrelating information management functions. It can be
applied to the areas of business-IT alignment and sourcing, and can
be of use when considering IT governance. It offers a high level view
of the entire scope of information management; its main application
is in the analysis of organization and responsibilities.

AIM can be used to support strategic discussions in three
different ways, as shown in the Figure:

- Descriptive, orientation – the framework offers a map of the
  entire information management domain, and can be used for
  positioning specific information management processes in the
  organization

- Specification, design – the framework can be used to re-organize the information management organization, e.g. to specify the role of the Chief Information Officer (CIO) or determine the responsibilities of the retained organization in the case of outsourcing
- Prescriptive, normative – the framework can be used as a diagnostic instrument to find gaps in an organization's information management, and is specifically aimed at identifying missing interrelationships between the various components of the framework

On the horizontal axis, the framework distinguishes three domains of governance:

1. Business – this domain comprises all standard business functions such as management, HR, resources and processes.
2. Information and Communication (information domain) – this domain describes how information and communication supports the business. In this domain, business requirements are translated into the IT (technology) capabilities that are needed to support the business.
3. Technology (IT domain) – this domain specifically describes the development and management of IT solutions.

The vertical axis describes the three levels of governance:
- Strategy (scope, core competences and governance)
- Structure (architecture and competences)
- Operations (processes and skills)

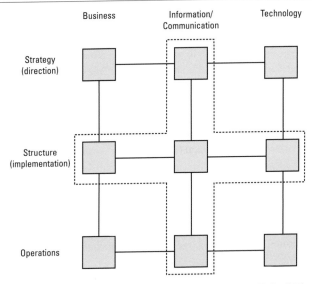

Abcouwer, Maes and Truijens (1997)

Figure: The AIM or Nine Square framework

AIM (originally known as the nine square framework) connects
the two dimensions of management and information as the
central components for Information Management. The dotted
line demarks the scope of Business-IT alignment.

4 Target audience
The framework was developed for information managers,
enterprise architects and IT architects.

5 Scope and constraints
The scope of the framework is the information management
domain.

This framework enables discussions on the topic of business and IT alignment, but it does not provide information on how organizations can actually achieve better communications between business and IT. The framework is not a method, and cannot be used in a descriptive way; however, it can be a useful addition to enterprise architecture frameworks such as TOGAF®.

6 Relevant website

www.primavera.fee.uva.nl (Dutch only)

ASL®

1 Title/current version

ASL®2 (Application Services Library)

2 The basics

ASL (Application Services Library) is a framework and collection of best practices for application management.

3 Summary

ASL (Application Services Library) was developed by a Dutch IT service provider, PinkRoccade, in the 1990s and was made public in 2001. Since 2002 the framework and the accompanying best practices have been maintained by the ASL BiSL Foundation. The current version is ASL2, published in the Netherlands in 2009.

ASL is concerned with managing the support, maintenance, renewal and strategy of applications in an economically sound manner. The library consists of a framework, best practices, standard templates and a self-assessment. The ASL framework provides descriptions of all the processes that are needed for application management.

The framework distinguishes six process clusters, which are viewed at operational, managing and strategic levels see Figure.

The *application support cluster* at the operational level aims to ensure that the current applications are used in the most effective way to support the business processes, using a minimum of resources and leading to a minimum of operational disruptions. The *application maintenance and renewal cluster* ensures that the applications are modified in line with changing requirements, usually as a result of changes in the business processes, keeping the applications up-to-date. The connecting processes form the bridge between the service organization cluster and the development and maintenance cluster.

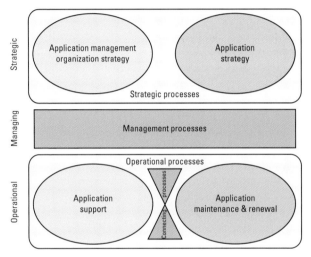

Figure: The ASL framework

The management processes ensure that the operational clusters are managed in an integrated way.

Finally, there are two clusters at the strategic level. The aim of the *application strategy cluster* is to address the long-term strategy for the application(s). The processes needed for the long-term strategy for the application management organization are described in the *application management organization strategy cluster.*

4 Target audience

The target audience for ASL consists of everyone who is involved in the development and management of applications: application support personnel, application architects and designers, programmers, testers, and managers with responsibility for application development or application management.

5 Scope and constraints

The scope of ASL is the support, maintenance, renewal, and strategy of applications, and the management of all related activities.

Strengths

- It offers a common language and conceptual framework for application management (maintenance and support)
- It provides an overview of all the activities (from operational to strategic) that are needed to keep applications up-to-date with the changing needs of the organization
- It is usable in various organizations
- It is owned and supported by a not-for-profit, vendor-independent foundation with participation by a wide range of organizations

Constraints

- ASL overlaps partially with other IT Service Management frameworks

6 Relevant website

www.aslbislfoundation.org

Business Relationship Management (BRM)

1 Title/definition

Business Relationship Management (BRM)

2 The basics

Business Relationship Management stimulates, surfaces and shapes business demand for a provider's products and services and ensures that the potential business value from those products and services is captured, optimized and recognized.

The concept of Business Relationship Management (BRM) is related to and employs the techniques and disciplines of Customer Relationship Management (CRM). However, while CRM most often refers to a company's external customers, the BRM typically deals with a company's internal *business partners* or an internal *provider's* products and/or services.

While BRM has its roots in CRM, it has come to mean different things to different people–often depending upon the specific industry context. For example, in banking and finance, the Business Relationship Manager manages and maintains current business relationships and seeks new accounts. Banking BRMs are typically responsible for a portfolio of small to mid-sized businesses. In other industries, the label "BRM" has come to be a euphemism for "account executive" or even "salesperson."

3 Summary

The BRM Discipline rests on solid research-based foundations verified and enhanced over a decade of successful implementations in leading organizations across the world. Proven to be equally effective for a wide range of internal providers including Human Resources, Finance, Legal, external service providers and others, BRM practices have enjoyed widespread adaption in IT. BRM implementations rate in IT services has quickened significantly, since 2011, when the BRM role and corresponding processes have been formalized as an Information Technology Infrastructure Library (ITIL®) best practice and an ISO/IEC 20000 IT Service Management international standard requirement.

The Practice of Business Relationship Management embodies a set of competencies (e.g. knowledge, skills, and behaviors) to foster an effective business value-producing relationship between a service provider and its business partners. These competencies can be leveraged through organizational *roles* (e.g. in an IT organization, the CIO typically has a role of BRM for the enterprise), a *discipline* (e.g. all business partner facing service provider roles should be skilled in Business Relationship Management), and an organizational *capability* (e.g. a service provider organization should be effective in shaping and channeling demand to the highest business value opportunities).

The BRM Role is a crucial link between a service provider and the business acting as a connector, orchestrator, and navigator between the service provider and one or more business units.

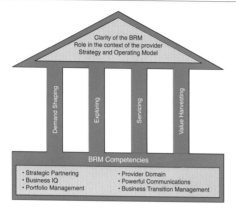

The House of BRM illustrates three key aspects of Business
Relationship Management:

1. The "foundation" supports the BRM role and ensures it has
   the *competencies* to be effective and deliver value to both the
   provider organization and its business partners.
2. The "pillars" define the BRM space in terms of Core BRM
   Disciplines: Demand Shaping, Exploring, Servicing and Value
   Harvesting.
3. The "roof" of the House of BRM protects Business
   Relationship Management as a key aspect of provider
   capability. It does this by ensuring clarity around how the
   role, discipline and organizational capability of Business
   Relationship Management in the context of the Provider
   Strategy and Operating Model.

Four Core BRM Disciplines

- **Demand Shaping** stimulates, surfaces and shapes business
  demand for provider services, capabilities and products.
  It ensures that business strategies fully leverage provider

capabilities, and that the provider service portfolio and capabilities enable business strategies. Most importantly, Demand Shaping is focused on optimizing the business value realized through provider services, capabilities and products—that low value demand is suppressed while higher value demand is stimulated.

- *Exploring* identifies and rationalizes demand. Business Relationship Management helps sense business and technology trends to facilitate discovery and demand identification. Exploring is an iterative and ongoing process that facilitates the review of new business, industry and technology insights with potential to create value for the business environment. The key benefit of this discipline is the identification of business value initiatives that will become part of the provider portfolio of services, capabilities and products.

- *Servicing* coordinates resources, manages Business Partner expectations, and integrates activities in accordance with the business partner-provider partnership. It ensures that business partner-provider engagement translates demand into effective supply requirements. Servicing facilitates business strategy, Business Capability Roadmapping, portfolio and program management.

- *Value Harvesting* ensures success of business change initiatives that result from the exploring and servicing engagements. Value harvesting includes activities to track and review performance, identify ways to increase the business value from business-provider initiatives and services, and initiates feedback that triggers continuous improvement cycles. This process provides stakeholders with insights into the results of business change and initiatives.

4   Target audience

Any business professional or organization wishing to better
stimulate, surface and shape business demand for a provider's
products and services and ensure that the potential business
value from those products and services is fully captured,
optimized, and recognized.

5   Scope and constraints

With its focus on improving relationships among business
partners and maximizing business value, the principles of the art
and practice of Business Relationship Management are equally
relevant to anyone engaged in business—anyone from rank-and-
file employees to C-level executives. If maximizing business value
realization of resources spent is of any concern to you, BRM is a
discipline, which will help you to achieve your objectives.

Constraints

Although 2011 editions of ISO/IEC 20000 standard and
ITIL® best practices rekindled the public interest in Business
Relationship Management, their scope is limited to IT and the
guidance they provide is most effective in the initial stages of
BRM capability implementations and at the lower levels of its
maturity. To be truly successful in rolling out and maximizing the
potential of BRM capability, organizations should follow a much
more holistic approach, one developed, promoted, and constantly
refined by Business Relationship Management Institute.

Relevant links website

Official Business Relationship Management Institute's
website:www.brminstitute.org
APMG is responsible for facilitating the delivery of Business
Relationship Management Professional (BRMP®) training and
certification.

CMMI®

1 Title/current version

CMMI® (Capability Maturity Model® Integration) Version 1.3.

2 The basics

CMMI is an internationally recognized process improvement approach that helps organizations to identify where to focus their improvement efforts along an evolutionary maturity path from ad hoc and chaotic to mature disciplined processes.

3 Summary

CMMI is owned and supported by the Carnegie Mellon® Software Engineering Institute (SEI). Version 1.0 of the CMM for Software (SW-CMM) was published in 1991; it was upgraded to CMM Integration (CMMI) in 2000 and the current version is Version 1.3, released in November 2010. An important change in Version 1.3 is the addition of Agile.

CMMI integrates traditionally separate organizational functions, sets process improvement goals and priorities, provides guidance for quality processes, and provides a point of reference for appraising current processes. The CMMI models are collections of best practices that help organizations to improve their processes:

- The CMMI for Acquisition (CMMI-ACQ) model provides guidance on managing the supply chain to meet the needs of the customer
- The CMMI for Development (CMMI-DEV) model supports improvements in the effectiveness, efficiency, and quality of product and service development

- The CMMI for Services (CMMI-SVC) model provides guidance on establishing, managing, and delivering services that meet the needs of customers and end users
- The People CMM provides guidance on managing and developing the workforce

An organization appraises its processes against the CMMI best practices:

- To determine how well its processes compare to CMMI best practices, and to identify areas where improvement can be made
- And/or to inform external customers and suppliers of how well its processes compare to CMMI best practices
- And/or to meet the contractual requirements of one or more customers

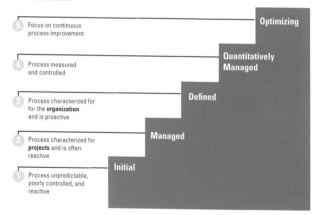

Figure: CMMI maturity levels
Source: SCI

Organizations can use a **staged** approach to appraisal to identify process maturity levels from 1 to 5 (see Figure). They can also

take a more flexible **continuous** approach to appraisal, measuring capability maturity in individual process areas. The appraisal results can then be used to plan process improvements for the organization.

4 Target audience

Managers responsible for process improvement programmes, project managers, process improvement specialists, project team members, appraisals teams.

5 Scope and constraints

- CMMI applies to teams, work groups, projects, divisions, and entire organizations
- CMMI works best in combination with Agile, Scrum, ITIL®, Six Sigma, COBIT®, ISO 9001, RUP®, or Lean
- Provides a common, integrated vision of improvement – or can focus on a specific process area
- Generic descriptions based on industry best practice
- Supporting guidance such as roadmaps help to interpret generic models for specific circumstances

Constraints:

- Aiming for higher maturity levels that will not achieve increased business benefits
- Rigid adherence to a staged approach– trying to move every project in the organization to the next level of maturity can be costly and time-consuming
- Failing to interpret the generic descriptions appropriately for the specific needs of the organization

6 Relevant websites

www.sei.cmu.edu/cmmi

COBIT®

1 Title/current version
COBIT®5

2 The basics
Originally designed for auditors to audit the IT organization, COBIT 5 (Control Objectives for Information and Related Technology) is about linking business goals to IT objectives (note the linkage here from vision to mission to goals to objectives). COBIT 5 (launched April 2012) provides metrics and maturity models to measure whether or not the IT organization has achieved its objectives. Additionally, COBIT identifies the associated responsibilities of the business process owners as well as those of the IT process owners.

3 Summary
COBIT is owned and supported by ISACA. It was released in 1996; the current Version 5.0 (April 2012) brings together COBIT 4.1, Val IT 2.0 and Risk IT frameworks.

The COBIT 5 principles and enablers are generic and useful for enterprises of all sizes, whether commercial, not-for -profit or in the public sector (Figures 1 and 2).

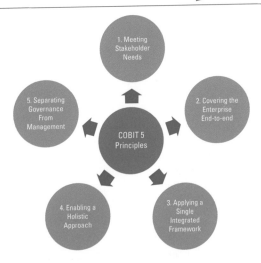

Figure 1: The COBIT 5 Principles

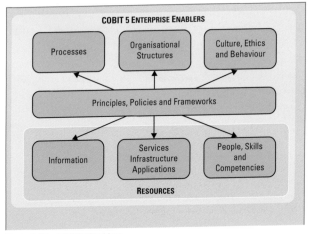

Figure 2: The COBIT 5 Enablers

The process reference model defines and describes in detail a number of governance, and management processes. It represents all the processes normally found in an organization relating to IT activities, thus providing a common reference model understandable to operational IT, and business managers, and their auditors/advisors. The process reference model divides the processes of organization IT into two domains: governance and management.

COBIT 5 provides a set of 36 governance and management processes within the framework.

The governance domain contains five governance processes; within each process, evaluate, direct, and monitor practices are defined.
- EDM1: set and maintain the governance framework
- EDM2: ensure value optimisation
- EDM3: ensure risk optimisation
- EDM4: ensure resource optimisation
- EDM5: ensure stakeholder transparency

The four management domains, in line with the responsibility areas of plan, build, run, and monitor (PBRM) provide end-to-end coverage of IT.
- Align, plan, and organize
- Build, acquire, and implement
- Deliver, service, and support
- Monitor, evaluate, and assess

A casual look at the four management domains of COBIT 5 rapidly illustrates its direct relationship with ITIL.
- The align, plan, and organize domain relates to the service strategy and design phases
- The build, acquire, and implement domain relates to the service transition phase
- The deliver, service, and support domain relates to the service operation phase
- And finally, the monitor, evaluate, and assess domain relates to the continual service improvement phase

All aspects of COBIT 5 are in line with the responsibility areas of plan, build, run and monitor. In other words, COBIT 5 follows the PDCA cycle of Plan, Do, Check, and Act. COBIT has been positioned at a high level, and has

been aligned and harmonized with other, more detailed, IT standards and proven practices such as COSO, ITIL, ISO 27000, CMMI, TOGAF and *PMBOK Guide*. COBIT 5 acts as an integrator of these different guidance materials, summarising key objectives under one umbrella framework that links the proven practice models with governance and business requirements.

4 Target audience

Senior business management, senior IT management and auditors.

5 Scope and constraints

COBIT provides an 'umbrella' framework for IT governance across the whole of an organization. It is mapped to other frameworks and standards to ensure its completeness of coverage of the IT management lifecycle and support its use in enterprises using multiple IT-related frameworks and standards.

Some strong points are:
- Value creation through effective governance, management enterprise information and technology (IT) assets
- Business user satisfaction with IT engagement and services by enabling business objectives
- Compliance with relevant laws, regulations and policies

Constraints:
- Treating COBIT as a prescriptive standard when it should be interpreted as a generic framework to manage IT processes and internal controls. Key themes from COBIT must be tailored to the specific governance needs of the organization

- Lack of commitment from top management – without their leadership and support, the IT control framework will suffer and business alignment of IT risks will not happen
- Underestimating the cultural change – COBIT is not just about the technical aspects of IT. The organization needs to have a good understanding of the governance controls for the IT risks

6 Relevant website

www.isaca.org

DevOps

1 Title / definition

DevOps

2 The Basics

Literally speaking, DevOps is a joining of development and operations. However, to understand what it truly is, some background is required on its origins. Ignited by Patrick Debois and Andrew Clay Shafer, discussing agile infrastructure at the Agile 2008 conference, it really caught fire after the first DevOps Days in Ghent one year later. Since then, tens of DevOps Days have been organized by a rapidly growing, hands-on community of IT professionals from both development and operations. It has led to a worldwide, bottom-up movement to enable a fast and resilient delivery of IT services. Along with this relevant movement automatically comes the inevitable desire to define and scope DevOps. Leading to semantic, even religious discussions, which in fact do not contribute to its goal (agility, collaboration and empathy across the IT value chain). So, without trying to ringfence it, DevOps aims at an organizational mindset for continuously improving value from the digital value chain by enabling cross-functional collaboration on process, technology and behavior level.

3 Summary

Organizations worldwide have adopted Lean and Agile ways of working to cope with their current disruptive markets. Lean Startup principles are adopted by large multinational corporations, and Agile methodologies have outgrown the IT department, towards primary processes in lawyer firms, schools and construction agencies. This, however, does not

say that these organizations actually bring new or adapted
software to production with the required speed and frequency.
Predominantly during this final step (often referred to as "the last
mile") the delivery hampers. The root cause? The organization
has too many silos, which are not (enough) connected.

The problem

Who hasn't seen them: IT departments where designers,
developers, testers, support and operations live in splendid
isolation from each other, with a minimal level of collaboration.
The designers cherish their own requirements and methodologies, developers work on their code (possibly in Scrum teams),
after which the results are pulled through the test factory, in
order to be thrown over the operations wall at the end. Products,
as delivered by the development teams (Scrum has named these
"potentially shippable products", or PSP), pile up in front of
operations' doorstep. By the way, using the PSP term consistently
in Scrum implementation worldwide, has contributed greatly
to the divergence of responsibility in the value chain. After all,
from the (Scrum) developer point of view, their job was "done"
once it was potentially shippable, hence on a pallet, waiting to be
shipped. At that time, it still does not delivery any value at all!
But the developer considered it done, as their work was done. No
relation to value whatsoever.

And when these product increments are eventually implemented
in a large release, it takes unacceptably long before errors can be
related to their source. Integration problems don't come to the
surface before the tester is running the acceptance tests. And
what about the customer satisfaction, if users are constantly faced
with delays and unavailabilities? In short, DevOps addresses the
need for higher user satisfaction, a dynamic balance between

value and risks, shorter time to market, and more efficiency in the end-to-end chain through cross-functional collaboration.

The Three Ways

As beautifully illustrated in the DevOps bible "The Phoenix Project", the value IT can deliver to an organization is completely dependent on its ability to make the organization collaborate as a whole. Although the name suggests only Development (Dev) and Operations (Ops) will more closely collaborate, the essence is much broader than just that. Bringing together Dev and Ops is referred to as "DevOps Lite" (after Patrick Debois), whereas true DevOps also entails the integration of crucial roles such as the business, testing/QA and security. This holistic thinking is the first principle (The First Way) of DevOps.

Besides that, it is considered fundamental to DevOps to not only have (mostly Agile) development teams deliver "potentially shippable products", but to have the target deployment environments available as well (provisioning). Clearly this is where DevOps takes Agile implementations one step further, thereby providing the IT organization more valuable feedback (The Second Way) on the quality of the delivered products. Surely automation plays an essential role here. Without a high degree of automation, it is virtually impossible to provision and synchronize (DTAP) environments in a fast and standardized way.

Probably the most fundamental shift which is part of the DevOps way of working, is the way errors and risks are dealt with. Traditional organizations tend to have a cultural heritage where errors are being punished, hence covered up. DevOps organizations assume that errors and experiments are excellent, as they improve the organization's resilience (The Third Way).

It enhances the organizational capability to learn, moving these types of organizations towards a state of "antifragility" (Nicholas Taleb). They are known for their ability to absorb disturbances, even grow from them, and continuously adapt to changing circumstances.

Relations

The revolutionary aspect of DevOps is not about the individual components it touches. It is the contextual combination and application of these frameworks, methods and movements. The following essential relations are identified in relation to DevOps:

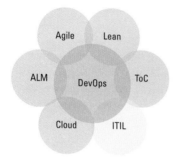

Agile: Many of the principles applied in organizations that have adopted DevOps, concur with the Agile principles. Think of short feedback loops, minimizing unit size and fast flow of planned work.

Lean: The Lean way of thinking is not only applicable to the factory floor. Lean elements such as Voice of the Customer, Flow, Pull and Kaizen are used more and more in IT organizations. Waste is reduced and errors are identified and solved at the source ("no defects downstream").

Theory of Constraints: This methodology, related to Lean, is characterized by the elimination of bottlenecks. By consistently searching for essential limitations in your organization's product and service flows, these constraints (or bottlenecks) can be taken away adequately.

ITIL: Without a doubt, ITIL also plays a significant role in DevOps organizations. If well applied, the introduction of Agile and Lean principles and instruments in the entire IT delivery chain (so including operations and support) account for faster and more flexible service management processes. Take Configuration Management, which is crucial in DevOps in sharing information between several roles and domains.

Cloud: Many organizations have started their transformation to the cloud, either partly or full blown. Cloud technology enables fast provisioning , adjustment (scaling up/down) and synchronization of (DTAP) environments and in automating several build, integration, test or deployment tasks.

Themes
Typical patterns we encounter in DevOps environments include:

- **Continuous Delivery**
  Delivery pipelines are automated, resulting in practices like continuous integration, continuous deployment, automated testing.
- **Software Defined Anything**
  Servers, even entire networks are software defined nowadays. Physical, on-premise hardware is replaced by virtual machines and containers.

- **Agile architecture**
  Huge monolythic applications are replaced by microservices, enabling fast feedback, low regression testing and maximizing the use of market standardization.
- **Service flow**
  By using Lean processes, a value-driven approach challenging the end-to-end performance of the value stream, continuously optimizing batch size and queues.
- **Functional vs non-functional requirements**
  A sound balance between functional and non-functional system behavior requires professional product ownership, but also built-in quality, security and monitoring.
- **Learning culture**
  Failure is regarded as valuable learning points instead of opportunities for punishment, resulting in blameless postmortems and rewards for positive experimental behavior.

4 Target audience

DevOps as a theme is relevant for everyone involved in the digital value chain. Whether you are from HR, selling mortgages, develop software, write testscripts or operate infrastructure in the cloud.

5 Recommended website

Whitepaper Gene Kim: https://www.thinkhdi.com/~/media/HDICorp/Files/White-Papers/whtppr-1112-devops-kim.pdf
Blog Rob England: http://www.itskeptic.org/content/define-devop

e-CF

1 Title/current version
e-CF (European e-Competence Framework) - Version 3.0.

2 The Basics
The European e-Competence Framework, e-CF, is a reference framework for competences applied within the IT sector and a common language for IT-related knowledge, skills and attitudes.

3 Summary
The e-CF has been developed by the Workshop on IT Skills of the European Committee for Standardization (CEN), with contributions from a large number of IT and HR experts. The development of the e-CF started in 2005 after recommendations from the European e-Skills Forum that national IT framework stakeholders and IT experts should consider developing a European e-competence framework. With the introduction of Version 3.0 in 2014 the CEN started the process to make the e-CF a European standard.

A competence is defined in the e-CF as a *demonstrated ability to apply knowledge, skills and attitudes to achieving observable results*.
Each of the 40 competences in e-CF 3.0 is described in four so called 'dimensions':
1. The e-Competence Area taken from a simple IT process model: Plan – Build – Run – Enable – Manage
2. A Generic Description in terms of the behavior showing the competence and the expected contribution at the workplace
3. Proficiency Levels based on a mix of:
   - autonomy (from 'being instructed' to 'making choices')

- context complexity (from 'structured/predictable' to 'unstructured/unpredictable')
- behavior (from 'able to apply' to 'able to conceive')
4. Knowledge and Skills examples that may be relevant for competence performance as described in dimensions 2 and 3

The e-CF proficiency levels, 1 to 5, are very similar to the levels 3 to 8 of the European Qualification Framework (EQF) used in formal education. For most competences in the e-CF only two or three levels are defined.

The e-CF is published by the CEN IT Skills Workshop as a CEN Workshop Agreement (CWA) and consists of four parts:
- Part 1 is the standard itself
- Part 2 contains guidance on the use of the standard
- Part 3 documents how the e-CF was developed
- Part 4 illustrates the application of e-CF in practice by providing 15 case studies

4 Target audience
The framework provides an international tool for:
- IT practitioners and managers, with clear guidelines for their competence development
- Human resources managers, enabling the anticipation and planning of competence requirements
- Education, training and certification, enabling effective planning and design of IT curricula and assessment of professionals
- Policy makers, professional organizations and market researchers, providing a clear and Europe-wide agreed reference for IT professionalism, IT skills and competences in a long-term perspective

IT & IT management

(A – E)		e-1 to e-5, related to EQF levels 3–8				
		e-1	e-2	e-3	e-4	e-5
A. PLAN	A.1. IS and Business Strategy Alignment					
	A.2. Service Level Management					
	A.3. Business Plan Development					
	A.4. Product/Service Planning					
	A.5. Architecture Design					
	A.6. Application Design					
	A.7. Technology Trend Monitoring					
	A.8. Sustainable Development					
	A.9. Innovating					
B. BUILD	B.1. Application Development					
	B.2. Component Integration					
	B.3. Testing					
	B.4. Solution Deployment					
	B.5. Documentation Production					
	B.6. Systems Engineering					
C. RUN	C.1. User Support					
	C.2. Change Support					
	C.3. Service Delivery					
	C.4. Problem Management					
D. ENABLE	D.1. Information Security Strategy Development					
	D.2. IT Quality Strategy Development					
	D.3. Education and Training Provision					
	D.4. Purchasing					
	D.5. Sales Proposal Development					
	D.6. Channel Management					
	D.7. Sales Management					
	D.8. Contract Management					
	D.9. Personnel Development					
	D.10. Information and Knowledge Management					
	D.11. Needs Identification					
	D.12. Digital Marketing					
E. MANAGE	E.1. Forecast Development					
	E.2. Project and Portfolio Management					
	E.3. Risk Management					
	E.4. Relationship Management					
	E.5. Process Improvement					
	E.6. IT Quality Management					
	E.7. Business Change Management					
	E.8. Information Security Management					
	E.9. IS Governance					

Figure: Overview of the e-CF competences and proficiency levels

- Procurement managers, providing a common language for effective technical terms of reference in national and international bids

5 Scope and Constraints

The e-CF supports the definition of job roles, career paths, professional development plans, learning paths and qualifications based on a shared common language and competence structure. It allows detailed profiling by defining profiles combining various competences. Measurement and assessment of competence using the e-CF as a reference framework enables the identification of competence gaps at an individual, team or organizational level, and effective targeted training or recruitment.

Strengths
Where job titles and job descriptions rapidly become obsolete in the dynamic and complex environment of modern organizations, competence is recognized as a more stable basis expressing capabilities required in the workplace.

As a reference framework, the e-CF can be aligned with HR instruments already existing in an organization, including other competence frameworks.

Constraints
The e-CF descriptions of competences, describing behavior in the workplace, are easily misunderstood as describing roles in an organization. Using the e-CF, e.g. for role profiles, one has to keep in mind that the framework is just that: a framework. Guidance on how to use the framework can be found in Part 2, the User Guide.

6 Relevant websites

www.ecompetences.eu

ISM

1 Title

The ISM method Version 3

2 The Basics

All service delivery organizations have the same goals and are therefore capable of using the same basic IT processes. With only 6 fundamental processes, every IT-organization can do their work on A tactical and operational level.

IT Service management is more alive than ever. It's about organizing Service Delivery. It might have started with ITIL, but nowadays it includes ABC, agile, LeanIT, DevOps, OBM etc. Integrating all these meaningful designs and models into one solution wherein each can fulfill its necessary role is one of the exciting challenges for the coming years.

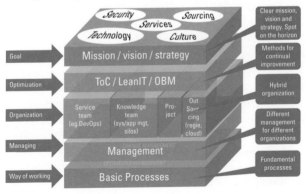

Processes are meant to support IT professionals in executing their profession, not to control them. Processes should follow and

support the natural professional behavior and increase flow and
quality. Staff and management should be able to use the model.

3 Summary

The ISM Method, first published in 2010, describes clearly the
need for a compact process model to support the professional IT
service delivery. The ISM model applies the lessons learned from
ITIL by reducing the amount of processes and translates them in
a complete and compact model.

The focus of ISM is on result, service delivery, and therefore the
model must be simple and applicable. Only applicable knowledge
is useful.

Service management is considered to be the profession that it
organizes the way in which IT departments work. Therefore
the ISM Method aligns all resources, People, Processes and
Products, that are necessary to realize operational excellence in a
process oriented way.

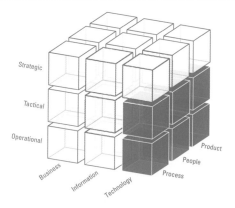

Organizational change is the cornerstone / backbone of the ISM Method. How to become an excellent service delivery organization. Leadership, clear distinction of roles, and especially a phased and structured approach to increase service excellence with a fundamental role of IT Management.

Other important elements are:
- Clear distinction of the position of Technical Management (the area of ISM®) and Information Management (the area of FSM®)
- The relation between People, Process and Product, the organizational resources
- The relation between process management and line management
- The ISM process model and the relation between the processes
- The fundamental role of the 6 basis processes, covering all activities on a tactical and operational level
- The emphasis on a phased implementation, introducing processes is changing the way of working

- phase I the installation of all the People, Process and
Product resources
- phase II implementation wherein an organization learns to
work with the processes and to continually improve
- Clear distinction between processes and functions
- The usage of clear definitions – more than 600 terms easily
explained

4 Target audience

IT Managers - who realize that excellent services are delivered
by well-organized teams wherein IT professionals closely
work together, and are guided by clear and compact processes.
Managers who realize that they have to facilitate the growth of
their staff and organization to a more mature and flexible level.

Process managers – who want their process to support the service
delivery, to become in control and not to control. Managers
that want to focus on flow and flexibility and not on designing
processes and tools.

Team leads – who want to facilitate their staff with proper
understanding of the value of process oriented working

IT professionals – Who want to professionalize their way of
working by using IT-processes to improve their performance

IT service management consultants – Who want to help
organizations to grow to service excellence by introducing
applicable processes

IT service management trainers – who want to train managers
and staff in modern service management

5 Scope and Constraints

The ISM Method combines best practices and a structured design. It's simple to choose to make it applicable and manageable for every IT department.

Strength
- Easy to apply
- Complete and compact on a tactical and operational level
- All resources covered and aligned (People, Process and Product)
- Free of organizational structures, re-organizations do not influence the processes
- ready for hybrid organizations wherein classical knowledge teams (silos), projects, outsourcing and service teams (like in DevOps) are combined.
- One size fits all
- Proper preparation for compliancy and security

Constraints
- Limited to IT management, information management is described in FSM (Functional Service Management)
- Limited in the way of organinzing the work / the way of working, technical skills are not part of the method
- Organizational structures are not included or prescribed, the model should fit in any organizational structure
- Although the method is complete and ready to use, growing to service excellence will still need a phased and persistent approach from all involved players

6 Relevant Websites

www.ismportal.com

ISO/IEC 20000

1 Title/current version

ISO/IEC 20000-1:2011 Standard for IT Service management

2 The basics

ISO/IEC 20000-1:2011 is a service management system (SMS) standard, which specifies requirements for the service provider to plan, establish, implement, operate, monitor, review, maintain and improve an SMS. This standard consists of several parts.

3 Summary

ISO/IEC 20000 is owned by the International Standards Organization (ISO) and the International Electrotechnical Commission (IEC). It is the international IT Service Management standard that enables IT organizations (whether in-house, outsourced or external) to ensure that their IT service management processes are aligned both with the needs of the business and with international best practice. It is based on and replaces BS15000, which has now been withdrawn.

ISO/IEC 20000 helps organizations benchmark how they deliver managed services, measure service levels and assess their performance. It is broadly aligned with, and draws strongly on, **ITIL**.

The standard has two main parts, both with the general title *Information technology - Service management,* which enable IT service providers to identify how to enhance the quality of service they deliver to their customers, both internal and external:

- **Part 1: Specification** (ISO/IEC 20000-1:2011) provides requirements for IT service management and is relevant to

those responsible for initiating, implementing or maintaining IT service management in their organization

- **Part 2: Code of practice** (ISO/IEC 20000-2:2005) represents an industry consensus on guidance to auditors and assistance to service providers planning service improvements or to be audited against ISO/IEC 20000-1:2011

The other parts provide additional guidance on a more detailed level for specific areas like: scope definition and applicability of ISO/IEC 20000-1 (part 3), Process reference model (part 4), Exemplar implementation plan for ISO/IEC 20000-1 (part 5).

ISO 20000 uses the process-based approach of other management system standards such ISO 27001:2005, ISO 9001:2008 and ISO 14001:2004, including the Plan-Do-Check-Act (PDCA) cycle and requirements for continual improvement.

Organizations can have their IT service management systems independently certified as conforming to the requirements of ISO/IEC 20000-1:2011.

ISO 20000-3 provides essential information on writing a scope for a service management system (SMS) as well as providing information on implementing an ISO/IEC 20000-1 SMS.

4 Target audience
IT service providers; internal IT units; auditors.

5 Scope and constraints
ISO/IEC 20000 is appropriate for IT service provider organizations. It is suitable for all industry sectors and all sizes of

organization except the very smallest (where a wide ranging ISO 9000 certification is more appropriate).

The traditional use of a formal standard is to achieve formal certification; it is also helpful as a benchmark and guide to implementing best practice processes. The inherent nature of its unambiguously expressed requirements allows meaningful period-by-period comparisons, which can deliver a measure of improvement in a service provider's processes. ISO 20000 can assist an organization in benchmarking its IT service management, improving its services, demonstrating an ability to meet customer requirements and create a framework for an independent assessment.

Constraints

To achieve wide and comprehensive coverage, the standard addresses only the generically valid core elements of the service management processes; it can never describe the full set of processes/procedures that an individual service provider will require to deliver effective and efficient, customer-focused services.

6 Relevant website

www.iso.org

ISO/IEC 27000

1 Title/current version

ISO/IEC 27000:2014 Standard for Information Security Management

2 The basics

ISO/IEC 27000 is a series of information security standards developed and published by ISO and IEC. These standards provide a globally recognized framework for best practices in Information Security Management.

3 Summary

The ISO/IEC 27000 series is owned by the International Standards Organization (ISO) and the International Electrotechnical Commission (IEC). ISO 27001 is a specification that sets out specific requirements, all of which must be followed, and against which an organization's Information Security Management System (ISMS) can be audited and certified.

All the other Standards in the ISO 27000 family are Codes of Practice; these provide non-mandatory best practice guidelines which organizations may follow, in whole or in part, at their own discretion.

Key concepts that govern the standards are:

- Organizations are encouraged to assess their own information security risks
- Organizations should implement appropriate information security controls according to their needs
- Guidance should be taken from the relevant standards
- Implement continuous feedback and use of the Plan, Do, Check, Act model

- Continually assess changes in the threats and risks to information security issues

The ISO 27000 standards family

ISO/IEC 27000 provides an overview of information security management systems, which form the subject of the information security management system (ISMS) family of standards, and defines related terms

ISO/IEC 27001:2013 — Information technology – Security Techniques –Information security management systems (ISMS) — Requirements, does not rely Plan-Do-Check-Act cycle, but has been updated in other ways to reflect changes in technologies and in how organizations manage information

ISO/IEC 27002:2013 — Code of practice for information security controls, this contains the good practice information security control objectives and controls

ISO/IEC 27003 — Information security management system implementation guidance for the ISO/IEC 27001

ISO/IEC 27004 — Information security management — Measurement

ISO/IEC 27005 — Information security risk management, aligned to ISO/IEC 31000

ISO/IEC 27006 — The accreditation Standard with guidance for bodies providing audit and certification of information security management systems

ISO/IEC 27007 — Guidelines for information security management systems auditing (focused on the management system)

ISO/IEC TR 27008 — Technical Report on guidance for auditors on ISMS controls (focused on the (technical) information security controls)

ISO/IEC 27010 — Information security management for inter-sector and inter-organizational communications

ISO/IEC 27011 — Information security management guidelines for telecommunications organizations based on ISO/IEC 27002

ISO/IEC 27013 — Guideline on the integrated implementation of ISO/IEC 27001 and ISO/IEC 20000-1 (IT service management/ITIL)

ISO/IEC 27014 — Information security governance,offers guidance on the governance of information security

ISO/IEC TR 27015 — Technical Reference, Information security management guidelines for financial services

ISO/IEC TR 27016 — covers the economics of information security management

ISO/IEC 27017 — covers the information security controls for cloud computing, based on the ISO/IEC 27002

ISO/IEC 27018 — Code of practice for protection of personally identifiable information (PII) in public clouds acting as PII processors

ISO/IEC TR 27019 — provides guiding principles based on ISO/IEC 27002 for information security management applied to process control systems as used in the energy utility industry

ISO/IEC TR 27023 — Information technology – Security techniques -- Mapping the revised editions of ISO/IEC 27001 and ISO/IEC 27002

ISO/IEC 27031 — Guidelines for information and communication technology readiness for business continuity

ISO/IEC 27032 — Guideline for cybersecurity

ISO/IEC 27033-1 — Network security – Part 1: Overview and concepts

ISO/IEC 27033-2 — Network security – Part 2: Guidelines for the design and implementation of network security

ISO/IEC 27033-3 — Network security – Part 3: Reference networking scenarios - Threats, design techniques and control issues

ISO/IEC 27033-5 — Network security – Part 5: Securing communications across networks using Virtual Private Networks (VPNs)

ISO/IEC 27034-1 — Application security – Part 1: Guideline for application security

ISO/IEC 27035 — Information security incident management

ISO/IEC 27036-1 — Information security for supplier relationships - Part 1: Overview and concepts

ISO/IEC 27036-2 — Information security for supplier relationships - Part 2: Requirements

ISO/IEC 27036-3 — Information security for supplier relationships - Part 3: Guidelines for information and communication technology supply chain security

ISO/IEC 27037 — Guidelines for identification, collection, acquisition and preservation of digital evidence

ISO/IEC 27038 — Information technology – Security techniques -- Specification for digital redaction

ISO/IEC 27039 — Information technology – Security techniques -- Selection, deployment and operations of intrusion detection systems (IDPS)

ISO/IEC 27040 — Information technology – Security techniques -- Storage security

ISO/IEC 27041 — guidance on assurance for digital evidence investigation methods

ISO/IEC 27042 — guidance on analysis and interpretation of digital evidence

ISO/IEC 27043 — guidance on incident investigation.

ISO 31000 — Risk management — Principles and guidelines

4 Target audience

All roles responsible for IT security management in an organization, IT security management professionals and auditors.

5 Scope and constraints

The family of ISO/IEC 27000 standards is broad in scope: they are applicable to any organization, in any sector, of any size.

Strengths

By aligning itself with an ISO/IEC standard, an organization can:

- Secure its own critical assets
- Manage levels of risks
- Improve and ensure customer confidence
- Avoid loss of brand damage, loss of earnings or potential fines
- Evolve its information security alongside technological developments

Constraints / Pitfalls

- Few organizations formally state the scope of their ISMS or document their risk assessment method and risk acceptance criteria in accordance with the standard
- Many organizations lack formal procedures for reporting security events, and mechanisms to quantify and monitor incidents
- Business continuity plans are often either absent or outdated, while continuity exercises are irregular and unrealistic
- Few organizations identify all the information security-relevant laws and regulations, and established mechanisms to stay up-to-date on changes

6 Relevant website

www.iso.org

ISO 38500

1 Title/current version

ISO/IEC 38500:2008 Corporate governance of information technology

2 The basics

ISO/IEC 38500:2008 provides guiding principles for directors of organizations (including owners, board members, directors, partners, senior executives, or similar) on the effective, efficient, and acceptable use of IT within their organizations.

3 Summary

ISO/IEC 38500:2008 is owned by the International Standards Organization (ISO) and the International Electrotechnical Commission (IEC). The standard helps to clarify IT governance from the top down by describing it as the means through which directors can demonstrate to all stakeholders and compliance bodies their effective stewardship over IT resources by ensuring that an appropriate governance and security framework exists for all IT activities as a result of covering the following principles.

The principles are:

- Responsibility – employees know their responsibilities both in terms of demand and supply of IT and have the authority to meet them
- Strategy – business strategies should be aligned with IT possibilities, and all IT within an organization should support the business strategies
- Acquisition – all IT investments must be made on the basis of a business case with regular monitoring in place to assess whether the assumptions still hold

- Performance – the performance of IT systems should lead to business benefits and therefore it is necessary that IT supports the business effectively
- Conformance – IT systems should help to ensure that business processes comply with legislation and regulations; IT itself must also comply with legal requirements and agreed internal rules
- Human behavior – IT policies, practices and decisions respect human behavior and acknowledge the needs of all the people in the process

The standard consists of three parts: Scope, Framework and Guidance.

4 Target audience

Senior managers; members of groups monitoring the resources within the organization; external business or technical specialists, such as legal or accounting specialists, retail associations, or professional bodies; vendors of hardware, software, communications and other IT products; internal and external service providers (including consultants); IT auditors.

5 Scope and constraints

ISO/IEC 38500:2008 applies to the governance of management processes (and decisions) relating to the information and communication services used by an organization. These processes could be controlled by IT specialists within the organization, or external service providers, or by business units within the organization. The standard is applicable in all types of private and public and not-for-profit organizations independent of their size and form and regardless of the extent of their use of IT.

Strengths

The primary advantage of the ISO/IEC 38500:2008 IT governance framework is to ensure that accountability is clearly assigned for all IT risks and activities. This specifically includes assigning and monitoring IT security responsibilities, strategies and behaviors so that appropriate measures and mechanisms are established for reporting on and responding to the current and planned use of IT – for example, meeting the latest data protection requirements for encryption of all portable devices such as laptops and memory sticks used to store and transmit personal data.

Constraints

- Outsourcing: some requirements are so specific to the managers of IT that they cannot be imposed on the managers of the company if their IT is outsourced. In cases such as these, requirements will need to be secured in the contract with the supplier of IT services
- Applying the standard in isolation: ISO 38500 is not 'one size fits all'. It does not replace COBIT, ITIL, or other standards or frameworks, but, rather, it complements them by providing a demand-side-of-IT-use focus

6   Relevant website

www.iso.org

IT-CMF

1 Title / definition

IT-CMF™ (Information Technology Capability Maturity Framework™)

2 The basics

Organizations, both public and private, are constantly challenged to be increasingly more agile, innovative and value-adding. CIOs are uniquely well-positioned to seize this opportunity and adopt the role of business transformation partner, helping their organizations to grow and prosper with innovative, IT-enabled products, services and processes. To succeed in this, however, the IT function needs to manage an array of inter-dependent but distinct disciplines.

In response to this need, the Innovation Value Institute, a cross-industry international consortium, developed the IT Capability Maturity Framework™ (IT-CMF™).

3 Summary

The IT Capability Maturity Framework™ (IT-CMF™) represents a suite of capabilities – Figure 1 – that help improve the management of IT to deliver higher levels of agility, innovation and value creation.

Figure 1: IT-CMF's Critical Capabilities

Each critical capability of IT-CMF consists of capability building blocks (CBBs), which are characterized by maturity levels, are evaluated by maturity questions and are improved by practices-outcomes-metrics (POMs). Figure 2 graphically illustrates the relationship amongst IT-CMF's principal components.

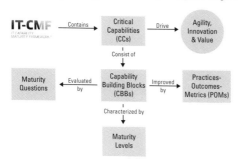

Figure 2: IT-CMF's Principal Components

4 Target Audience

Business and IT professionals seeking to harness the full potential of information technology in their organizations,

including CxOs, transformation change managers, IT strategy planners, general managers, and IT professionals aspiring to demonstrate leadership in adopting better approaches to managing technology for agility, innovation and value impact.

5 Scope and constraints

Framework Strengths

IT-CMF is:

- An integrated management toolkit covering more than 30 management disciples, with organizational maturity profiles, assessment methods, and improvement roadmaps for each.
- A coherent set of concepts and principles, expressed in business management terms, that can be used to guide discussions on setting goals and evaluating performance.
- A unifying (or umbrella) framework that complements other, domain-specific frameworks already in use in the organization, helping to resolve conflicts between them, and filling gaps in their coverage.
- Industry/sector and vendor independent. IT-CMF can be used in any organizational context to guide performance improvement.
- A rigorously developed approach, underpinned by the principles of Open Innovation and guided by the Design Science Research methodology, synthesizing leading academic research with industry practitioner expertise.

6 Considerations when using IT-CMF in your organization

- IT-CMF should be adopted at a senior management level, not just at the front-line staff/practitioner level, to realize the framework's full advantages.

- The framework delivers value through change. Committing to the required organizational change will help ensure expected outcomes are achievable.
- Appropriate capability selection and setting of maturity targets benefits from an appreciation of IT-CMF's critical capabilities, as well as a blended view across an organization's business strategy, IT posture and industry context.

7　Relevant Website

http://www.ivi.ie

ITIL®

1 Title/current version

ITIL (Information Technology Infrastructure Library) 2011
Edition

2 The basics

ITIL® is the most widely accepted approach to IT service
management in the world; it focuses on aligning IT services with
the needs of the business.

3 Summary

ITIL was created in the 1980s by the UK government's CCTA
(Central Computer and Telecommunications Agency) with the
objective of ensuring better use of IT services and resources.
ITIL is now owned by AXELOS: the current version is ITIL
2011 Edition (published July 2011), which updates ITIL v3.

ITIL advocates that IT services must be aligned with the needs
of the business and underpin the core business processes. It
provides guidance to organizations on how to use IT as a tool
to facilitate business change, transformation and growth. The
ITIL best practices are described in five core guides that map the
entire ITIL Service Lifecycle (see Figure).

- Service Strategy – understanding who the IT customers
  are, the service offerings to meet their needs, and the IT
  capabilities and resource to deliver the services
- Service Design – assures that new and changed services are
  designed effectively to meet customer expectations, including
  the technology, architecture and processes that will be required

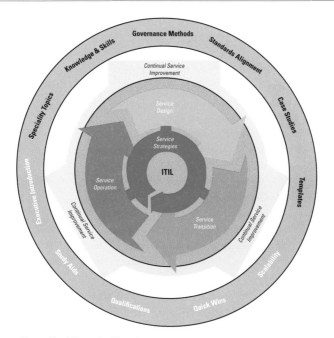

Figure: The ITIL service lifecycle
Source: AXELOS

- Service Transition – the service design is built, tested and moved into production to assure that the business customer can achieve the desired value
- Service Operation – delivers the service on an ongoing basis, including managing disruptions to service and supporting end-users
- Continual Service Improvement – measures and improves the service levels, the technology and the efficiency and

effectiveness or processes. It incorporates many of the same concepts articulated in the Deming Cycle of *Plan-Do-Check-Act*

4 Target audience

IT service providers and IT professionals in a wide range of roles.

5 Scope and constraints

The IT Service Management lifecycle is from service strategy through design, transition live operation and continuous improvement. Used in organizations large and small, across many different sectors worldwide.

Supported by quality services from a wide range of providers including examination institutes, accredited training providers and consultancies, software and tool vendors.

The updated guidance reflects the latest international standards relating to service management, including the 2011 edition of ISO/IEC 20000.

Strengths
- Universally accepted as the good practice guidance for IT Service Management, with process and service focus
- Supported by a vast community of ITIL practitioners, gathered around itSMF (IT Service Management Forum)

Constraints
When implementing ITIL-based IT Service Management processes in an IT provider organization, the most common pitfalls are:

- Narrow focus on the IT Unit's technology and process perspectives to gain incremental improvements (the organization should be embarking on a radical transformation journey to run IT as a business)
- Failing to do an assessment before implementing ITIL practices (identifying how the current organization structure compares to the ITIL framework and the changes that will be needed to the organization and its culture)
- Short term expectations (it is not a quick fix, achieved with just a handful of personnel trained and the purchase of some ITIL tools)

6 Relevant website

www.axelos.com

Lean IT

1 Title/current version
Lean IT

2 The basics
Lean IT is an extension of the Lean manufacturing and Lean services principles, applied in an IT environment. The approach is a way of thinking and acting, focusing heavily on organizational culture. Lean IT is associated with the development and management of Information Technology products and services. The central concern, applied in the context of IT, is the elimination of waste, where waste is work that adds no value to a product or service.

3 Summary
Lean IT focuses on maximizing customer value by minimizing waste, where *waste* is work that adds no value to a product or service. The mean focus is to achieve operational excellence through improved agility, service quality and process efficiency. It means building a customer and value-oriented culture in which employees engage in Lean IT processes. It also means involving all employees to continually improve services and preserve value with less effort and optimising IT operations and processes supporting the most business critical applications and services. Lean IT has a great impact on the culture of an organization with behavioral aspects such as empowering employees to involve them in the optimization of processes. The goal is to implement a rigorous problem solving process to achieve greater strategic and financial value.

There are many aspects of Lean IT within two primary dimensions:
- *Outward-facing Lean IT*: Engaging information, information systems, and the IT organization in partnership with the business

to continuously improve and innovate business processes and management systems

- *Inward-facing Lean IT*: Helping the IT organization achieve operational excellence, applying the principles and tools of continuous improvement to IT operations, services, software development, and projects

These two dimensions are not separate but complementary. They serve the ultimate objective of Lean transformation: creating value for the enterprise and its customers.

Lean IT is based on enterprise Lean principles, laying a solid foundation at the base. The three foundation elements support a strong social structure; constancy of purpose, respect for people and pursuit of perfection. The second layer is proactive behavior which means taking the initiative, assuming personal responsibility for the quality of the work and work environment. The third layer addresses awareness, with three essential perspectives embraced by the Lean enterprise: the voice of the customer, quality at the source, and systems thinking. The fourth layer focuses on flow, the uninterrupted progression of materials, services, and information. The fifth layer, the capstone of the principles, is culture, which represents an organization's shared beliefs and values, manifested as attitude and behavior. Culture is an outcome of behavioral change.

The principal focus of Lean IT is problem solving for the primary purpose of delivering value to the customer, achieved by the systematic elimination of waste throughout the value stream. A five-step thought process for implementing Lean thinking refers to:

- Specify value from the standpoint of the end customer
- Identify all the steps in the value stream, eliminating whenever possible those steps that do not create value

- Make the value-creating steps occur in tight sequence
- As flow is introduced, let customers pull value from the next upstream activity
- As value is specified, value streams are identified, wasted steps are removed, and flow and pull are introduced, begin the process again and continue it until a state of perfection is reached in which perfect value is created with no waste

4 Target audience

Any manager, specialist or team of any organization involved in IT process improvement of IT operations.

5 Scope and constraints

The scope of Lean IT is to establish a culture of continuous improvement to deliver IT operational excellence and business value to an organization. The IT organization is expected to "align with the business". That is, IT is supposed to enable business performance and innovation, improve service levels, manage change, take advantage of emerging technologies, and maintain quality and stability, all while steadily reducing operating costs. The scope of Lean IT must exceed a single function and should ideally be across a whole supply chain to obtain maximum benefit.

Constraints
When an enterprise begins a Lean transformation, too often the IT department is either left out or viewed as an obstacle. One of the hardest challenges a Lean IT team will face is the degree to which individual successes will invariably uncover new problems and greater challenges. This depends on the maturity of the business and the IT organization,

6 Relevant website

www.lean.org

SAF

1 Title

Service Automation Framework (SAF)

2 The Basics

Service Automation – the concept of delivering services through smart technology – is a rapidly growing area of interest for most organizations. Companies such as Spotify, Netflix and Uber (whom deliver 100% automated services) have proven that organizations can achieve rapid growth and gain a competitive advantage by relying on Service Automation.

Since Service Automation is a new topic, there has not a lot of (practical) information available on how organizations can set up Service Automation in their organizations. The Service Automation Framework® provides a step-by-step approach that illustrates how organizations can digitize their service offering in a methodical way. The corresponding certification scheme was developed for individuals and teams who aim to demonstrate their proficiency in the methodical steps of the Service Automation Framework. Additionally, the certification scheme provides a consistent starting point for organizations who want to start digitizing their service offering.

3 Summary

The Service Automation Framework consists of six main building blocks that can be divided into the 'heart' (focused on design) and the 'brain' (focused on delivery), which are both equally important in delivering automated services:

1. **User:** The building block that defines the key characteristics of the groups of people a service provider aims to serve;

2. **Service Design:** The business function that designs and

defines the service offering of a service provider. It is the concretization of the service concepts into an actual design, including the relevant support structures and digital interfaces;

3. **Technology:** The building block that defines the setup and usability of the digital interfaces, connecting service providers with their users;

4. **Automated Deployment:** The processes that enable a user to start using a service based on his or her own action;

5. **Service Delivery Automation:** The processes that enable a user to change or resolve any aspect of the service based on his or her own action;

6. **Serendipity Management:** The processes that facilitate a planned and continuous approach in order to constantly exceed the expectations of users.

Each of the six building blocks form an essential step in design and delivery of automated services.

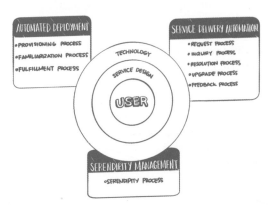

In addition to the six building blocks of SAF, the seven Service Automation Framework Techniques can be considered as a step-by-step plan that organizations can use to adopt Service Automation. Each of the seven SAFTs discuss in detail what techniques an organization should use to design and deliver automated services:

1. **SAFT1 – Building User Groups and User Characteristics:**
   In order to deliver 'valuable' services, it is necessary to understand the Service Perception of individual users. SAFT 1 provides the techniques to build the User Groups and User Characteristics that shape the Service Perception.

2. **SAFT2 – Translating User Profiles into User Action:**
   In order to ensure that services meet or exceed user requirements or expectations, service providers need to understand the needs and triggers that initiate service requests. SAFT2 provides the techniques to translate User Profiles into User Actions, keeping in mind the psychographic criteria that determine the overall UX.

3. **SAFT3 – Compose the Service Automation Blueprint**:
   The SAF Canvas enables the composition of a Service Automation Blueprint which outlines the 'ultimate User Experience' for a specific service and a specific User Group.

4. **SAFT4 – Technology Interface Modeling**:
   The goal of Technology Interface Modeling is to design a Self-Service Portal (e.g. the technology interface) based on industry best practices.

5. **SAFT5 – Implement Automated Deployment Processes:**
   The goal of this exercise is to apply the three processes of Automated Deployment (Provisioning Process, Familiarization Process and Fulfillment Process) into your own organization.

6. **SAFT6 – Implement Service Delivery Automation Processes**:
   The goal of this exercise is to apply the five processes of
   Service Delivery Automation (Request, Inquiry, Resolution,
   Upgrade and Feedback Process) into your own organization.

7. **SAFT7 – Surprise your user with Serendipity Management:**
   The goal of this exercise is to apply Serendipity Management to
   transform your organization's customers into long-term fans.

Through the chapters of the Service Automation book, each
of the seven Service Automation Framework Techniques is
illustrated using the case study of the Swan Hotel Group.

4 Target audience

Service Automation is a growth market across the entire world.
Whereas the competition in traditional Service Management
products is fierce, the SAF product allows training organizations
to showcase their innovative spirit and the opportunity to claim
a part of the Service Automation market in their respective
regions.

The Service Automation Framework is primarily intended for
individuals and organizations in the service industry, who can
gain a competitive advantage by digitizing their existing service
portfolio. Examples of industries that the SAF is especially
suitable for include the Finance, Insurance, Healthcare and
Government sectors.

5 Scope

The Service Automation Framework book covers the necessary
steps to digitize the service offering of organizations and provides
guidance on the 7 Service Automation Framework Techniques.

The key benefit of the book and corresponding certification is that is provides knowledge and practical tools that can be used in practice after reading the book.

6   Relevant Website

http://www.apmg-international.com/en/qualifications/SAF

Scrum

1 Title/current version

Scrum

2 The basics

Scrum is an iterative, incremental framework for project management often deployed in Agile software development.

3 Summary

Scrum is an Agile method (an iterative and incremental approach) for completing complex projects. Scrum was originally formalized for software development projects, but works well for any complex, innovative scope of work.

Why is it called Scrum?

When Jeff Sutherland created the scrum process in 1993, he borrowed the term 'scrum' from an analogy put forth in a 1986 study by Takeuchi and Nonaka, published in the Harvard Business Review. In that study, Takeuchi and Nonaka compare high-performing, cross-functional teams to the scrum formation used by Rugby teams.

Source: www.Scrumalliance.org

The Scrum Guide is the official Scrum Body of Knowledge. It was written by Ken Schwaber and Jeff Sutherland, co-creators of Scrum. The current version is Scrum Guide Version 2013.

The Scrum framework is summarized in the Sprint Cycle
(see Figure).

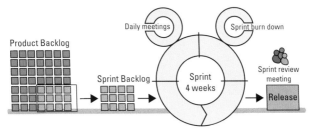

Figure: Scrum Sprint Cycle

A Sprint Cycle consists of the following steps:

– A Product Owner creates a prioritized wish-list called a
  Product Backlog.
– During Sprint planning, the team pulls a small chunk from
  the top of that wish-list, a Sprint Backlog, and decides how to
  implement those pieces.
– The team has a certain amount of time, a Sprint, to complete
  its work – usually two to four weeks – but meets each day to
  assess its progress (daily Scrum).
– The Sprint Burn Down chart shows implementation progress
  during a single Sprint.
– Along the way, the ScrumMaster keeps the team focused on
  its goal.
– At the end of the Sprint, the work should be potentially
  ready to hand to a customer, put on a store shelf, or show to a
  stakeholder.
– The Sprint ends with a Sprint Review and retrospective.
– As the next Sprint begins, the team chooses another chunk of
  the Product Backlog and begins working again.

The cycle repeats itself until sufficient items in the Product Backlog have been completed, the budget is depleted, or a deadline arrives. Which of these milestones marks the end of the work is entirely up to that specific project. No matter which impetus stops work, Scrum ensures that the most valuable work has been completed when the project ends.

The two main roles in Scrum are the Product Owner, who represents the customer and manages all requirements (adds requirements with a detailed description, prioritizes requirements and plans releases); and the ScrumMaster, who helps the team to follow Scrum process. The ScrumMaster facilitates the daily Scrum meetings, manages any problems, supports the Product Owner, and removes obstacles to team progress.

4 Target audience
Any member of a project team.

5 Scope and constraints
The scope of Scrum was originally intended for software development projects, but it is now also used for delivering any kind of complex projects.

Strengths
- Productivity increases (from 10% to 400% depending on team, environment, project, Agile experience, etc.)
- Continuous development process improvement
- Communication improvement inside development team and between Scrum team and customer
- Minimized time-to-market via frequent releases

Constraints

- Requires a lot of preparation/planning
- Focus on supporting tools
- Does not work well if team culture does not allow for roles as required in a cross functional team

6 Relevant website

www.scrum.org

SFIA

1 Title/current version

SFIA (Skills Framework for the Information Age) – Version 6
(released June 2015)

2 The basics

SFIA, the Skills Framework for
the Information Age, describes
skills required by professionals
in roles involving information
and communications technology.
First published in 2003, and
regularly updated, SFIA has
become the globally accepted
common language for the skills
and competencies required in the
digital world. The collaborative
development style involves open

consultation and input from people
with real practical experience of skills management in corporate
and educational environments. That is what sets SFIA apart
from other, more theoretical, approaches and has resulted in the
adoption of SFIA by organisations and individuals in nearly 200
countries.

3 Summary

SFIA is a practical resource for people who manage or work
in information systems-related roles of any type. It provides
a common reference model in a two-dimensional framework
consisting of skills on one axis and seven levels of responsibility
on the other. It describes professional skills at various levels of

competence. It also describes generic levels of responsibility, in terms of Autonomy, Influence, Complexity and Business Skills.

SFIA is updated frequently to remain in step with user needs and current thinking about information age capabilities.

A common language for skills in the digital world
SFIA gives individuals and organisations a common language to define skill, abilities and expertise in a consistent way. Clear language, avoiding technical jargon and acronyms, makes SFIA accessible to all, including Human Resources and Learning and Development professionals. It can solve some of the common translation issues that hamper communication and effective partnerships within organisations and mixed teams.
It helps describe business needs and to assess your workforce's ability to meet those needs.

By defining core competencies as professional standards, SFIA helps organisations create roadmaps and development plans where both they and their employees can recognise a pathway to success and improvement.

With the widespread use of SFIA today, this consistent approach aligns the way recruitment seeks talent with the way an individual can demonstrate the right fit for the right role.

And consistency means that SFIA works well for both large and small organisations: they share an approach, a vocabulary, and a focus on skills and capability.

SFIA fits in with your way of doing things. It does not define organisational structures, roles or jobs; it provides clear

descriptions of skills and levels of responsibility. The very structure of SFIA makes it a flexible resource which can be adopted and adapted to work in a range of HR systems and people-management processes.

4 Target audience

Individuals can map their current skills and experience, identify their goals, and plan their professional development journey. The mapping of higher-education courses, qualifications, professional memberships, and training courses helps individuals and their managers to choose the right actions and activities to support the development they need. SFIA can help in the creation of Job/ Position Descriptions and in advertising vacancies, and helps individuals to identify opportunities which match their skills and experience.

Organisations use SFIA for overall resource management. It can be used to quickly provide a baseline of the capability of the organisation, specific departments, teams, professional communities or individuals, and to identify skills gaps. SFIA describes the skills and levels of competency needed to operate effectively – ensuring that individuals can do their jobs properly, supporting the achievement of business and customer outcomes. Organisation structures, salary banding and benchmarking can be aligned to SFIA, facilitating a link to the skills and experience, focusing on the required capabilities and the value delivered.

During **Recruitment** SFIA helps employers to more accurately describe what they need, in language that potential employees understand. It helps move away from an over-reliance on certificates and qualifications that often only confirm a theoretical understanding of the relevant areas, and towards

specifying competency based on having the right skills and an appropriate level of experience and responsibility.

SFIA-based **role profiles** and **job descriptions** reduce business risk, increasing the chances of recruiting and developing individuals with the optimum mix of skills, at the right level. This is good for the organisation and the individual – it reduces the churn risk when individuals feel 'the job is not what they thought it would be', or the organisation discovers they haven't got the right set of skills to do the job effectively.

Education bodies, universities, colleges and **training** providers map their offerings to SFIA, to ensure the most appropriate courses and certifications are selected for individuals, providing the knowledge they need, so they can apply it to help develop the skills they require at the right level.

Professional bodies and membership organisations map SFIA to their membership levels, certifications, professional development and mentoring programmes. SFIA is used to identify suitable mentors, supporting knowledge and experience sharing and coaching activities.

Conference and event organisers can identify the target audience by mapping to SFIA levels of responsibility, skill categories or individual skills and levels – so individuals can select the sessions which best match their development needs.

The skills are grouped into categories and subcategories for convenience of use. Like previous versions, colour codes are used to help identify the category the skill has been classified under.

5 Scope and constraints

SFIA V6 contains 97 skills, each described at one or more of 7 levels of responsibility. To aid navigation, SFIA structuresthe skills into 6 categories, each with a number of sub-categories.

- Strategy and Architecture
- Change and Transformation
- Development and Implementation
- Delivery and Operation
- Skills and Quality
- Relationships and Engagement

SFIA Categories

These categories and sub-categories do not equate to jobs, roles, organisational teams, or areas of personal responsibility. The grouping is intended to assist people who are incorporating SFIA skills in role profiles or job descriptions, or who are building an organisation's competency framework. The categories and sub-categories do not have definitions themselves, they are simply logical structural containers to aid navigation – it is usual for a specific job description to comprise skills taken from multiple categories and sub-categories.

It also describes 7 generic levels of responsibility, in terms of Autonomy, Influence, Complexity, and Business Skills.

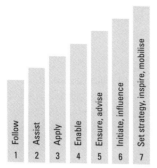

SFIA 7-levels of responsibility

The seven levels in SFIA are used in two key ways.

1. To provide generic levels of responsibility, with descriptions at each of the seven levels for the following attributes: AUTONOMY · INFLUENCE · COMPLEXITY · BUSINESS SKILLS

2. To reflect experience and competency levels within SFIA. The definitions describe the behaviours, values, knowledge and characteristics that an individual should have in order to be identified as competent at that level. Each level has a guiding word or phrase that acts as a brief indicator: FOLLOW · ASSIST · APPLY · ENABLE · ENSURE, ADVISE · INITIATE, INFLUENCE · SET STRATEGY, INSPIRE, MOBILISE

6 Relevant website

www.sfia-online.org

TRIM

1 Title

TRIM: The Rational IT Model – How to use IT Service
Management

2 The Basics

TRIM: The Rational IT Model describes IT service management
from an organizational point of view. Everything needs to be
connected to the purpose of an organizational unit and the
accountability of a role. All employees need to understand his or
hers contribution to the delivery of an IT service. It is comparable
to making a playbook for a sports team. And once this is in place,
processess will then be a tool to ensure that activities that need to
be done are easier to carry out. Instead of it being perceived as just
an administrative task, or even sometimes as an unpleasant job.

3 Summary

The purpose of TRIM: The Rational IT Model is not to replace
ITIL®, but to be a way to get ITI and IT service management
adopted within an organization. The model is complete and
describes the parts in such a way that you can understand IT,
even without prior ITILÒ knowledge. The model consists of the
fundamentals, namely the very basics for IT service management.
And the aim is that when it is in place and working, your
organization will be ready to really adopt and use more advanced
frameworks and models such as Lean, DevOps or any agile
methods.

The TRIM model is described in a book: *TRIM: The Rational
IT Model* Some of the topics in the book are:
• Functions

- Roles
- Governance model
- Operation
- Transition
- Delivery control
- Relations
- Strategy

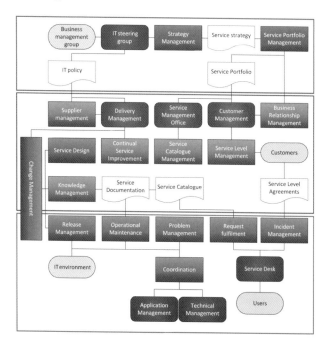

Providing a comprehensive, but still easy to understand, approach to IT service management and the needed components, TRIM: The Rational IT Model helps you to get an understanding of the

key to a service-oriented organization and provides a reference model for function, role, processes and governance to use in your work towards effective delivery of IT services.

4 Target audience

- CIO – Who are responsible for the IT Service delivery strategy
- **Managers** –who are primarily responsible for implementing and governing IT in their organizations and institutions.
- **IT Service Managers/Consultants** – that need a reference model for adopting IT Service Management
- **Executives**– who are primarily responsible for developing and/or approving IT strategy and then overseeing its implementation and governance (The "C" suite of Corporate Officers)
- **IT Practitioners** – that need a basic understanding of IT Service Management
- **Everyone within an IT organization** –who wants to know more about IT Service Management

5 Scope

The book covers all functions, roles and processes needed to get started and to use IT Service Management as a practice.

6 Relevant Website

http://www.opentrim.org/

VeriSM™

1 Title / Current version
VeriSM™

2 The Basics
Every organization is a service provider in today's market. Even organizations selling products need to add a level of service to them. Think of banking, insurance, civil services, but also the myriad of online shops where the physical product is a commodity and the service is the distinguishing characteristic of the organization. How do we best manage our services and keep our consumers happy? Recent years have seen an explosion of different service management practices, leaving organizations confused about the best way forward. VeriSM is a new approach to help you create a flexible operating model that will work for you, based on your desired business outcomes. VeriSM describes how an organization can define its service management principles, and then use a combination of management practices to deliver value

VeriSM describes a service management approach which is:
- **V**alue-driven
- **E**volving
- **R**esponsive
- **I**ntegrated
- **S**ervice
- **M**anagement

3 Summary
VeriSM describes a service management approach from the organizational level, looking at the end to end view rather than

focusing on a single department. Based around the VeriSM model, it shows organizations how they can adopt a range of management practices in a flexible way to deliver the right product or service at the right time to their consumers. VeriSM allows for a tailored approach depending upon the type of business you are in, the size of your organization, your business priorities, your organizational culture – and even the nature of the individual project or service you are working on.

Rather than focusing on one prescriptive way of working, VeriSM helps organizations to respond to their consumers and deliver value with integrated service management practices.

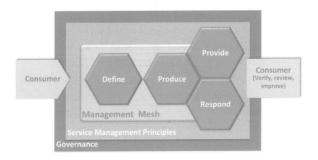

The VeriSM Model

In the model, governance overarches every activity, keeping a strong focus on value, outcomes and the organization's goals. Service management principles are then defined for the organization. These act as guardrails, to make sure that all products and services are aligned with the needs of the organization. Principles will be defined for areas including security, risk, quality and use of assets, and then communicated

to all of the staff who are involved with the development and operation of products and services.

The unique element of the VeriSM model is the management mesh. This provides a flexible approach that can be adapted depending on the requirements for a particular product or service. The mesh includes:

- Resources
- Environment
- Emerging technologies
- Management practices

For each product or service, these areas are considered and the mesh is flexed where necessary.

Let's take an example. A bank wants to create a mobile application that will let users send money to their friends with just one click. The mesh for this product could include agile development practices to get rapid feedback about the new product. The bank can use its capabilities and work in innovative ways, but they must still recognise the service management principles associated with security and risk.

4 Target Audience

VeriSM is essential reading for anyone who works with products and services. It will be of particular interest to:

- Managers – who want to understand how to leverage evolving management practices
- Service owners and service managers – who need to bring their skills up to date and understand how service management has changed
- Executives – who are accountable for effective service delivery
- IT professionals

- Graduates and undergraduates – who will be joining organizations and who need to understand the principles of service management
- Everyone within a service organization

5 Scope

VeriSM includes:

- Service culture
- Organizational context
- People/structure
- Service management challenges
- Processes, tools and measurement
- The VeriSM model
- Operating in a world of digital transformation
- Selecting and integrating management practices
- Progressive management practices including Lean, DevOps and Agile
- The impact of technology on service management
- Getting started

6 Relevant website

www.IFDC.global

project management

ICB4®

1 Title/definition
ICB4® IPMA Individual Competence Baseline, Version 4

2 The basics
The IPMA Individual Competence Baseline (ICB4) is the global standard for individual competences in project, programme and portfolio management.

3 Summary
The International Project Management Association (IPMA) is a leading worldwide not-for-profit project management association with more than 60 member associations. IPMA published the first official version of the ICB (Version 2.0) in 1999, with a small modification in 2001. Version 3 was published in 2007 and Version 4 in 2015.

A central concept of the ICB4 is the 'eye of competence', which represents the three management domains of project, programme, and portfolio management. Based on a generic model each individual has to have perspective competences that address the context of his or her project, programme or portfolio, people competences that address personal and social topics and practices competences that address the specific technical aspects for managing his or her project, programme or portfolio.

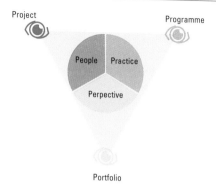

Figure 1: IPMA 'eye of competence'

The ICB4 defines 29 competence elements:
- 5 Perspective competence elements
- 10 People competence elements
- 14 Practice competence elements.

Each competence element consists of a definition, the purpose, a description of the content, knowledge areas, skills and a list of related competence elements as well as a set of key competence indicators with a description and measures.

IPMA offers a four level certification programme based on the IPMA Individual Competence Baseline (ICB4): IPMA level A-D.

4 Target audience

The target audience consists of project, programme and portfolio managers and staff as well as general managers, assessors, coaches, HR managers and trainers involved in project, programme and portfolio management. This list is by no means exhaustive.

5 Scope and constraints

The strength of the IPMA competence baseline is that it is a comprehensive inventory of competences an individual needs to have or to develop to successfully realise projects, programmes or portfolios. None of the other frameworks or methods for project, programme or portfolio management does this. The ICB4 framework is therefore most suitable as a reference model for the development and assessment of individual project, programme and portfolio managers. Further the ICB4 is applicable for all sectors and industries.

The ICB4 does not recommend or include specific methods or tools. Methods and tools may be defined by the organization. The project, programme or portfolio manager should choose appropriate methods and tools fit for the actual circumstances.

6 Relevant website

Official IPMA website: www.ipma.ch

ISO 21500

1 Title/current version

ISO 21500:2012 – Guidance on project management

2 The basics

ISO 21500 – Guidance on project management has been approved in an international ballot of participating national standards authorities. It provides a comprehensive and structured set of concepts and processes that are considered to form good practice in project management. Projects are placed in the context of programmes and project portfolios. Topics related to general management are addressed only within the context of project management. In some countries (eg. South Korea) it has already been declared as the standard for project management to which all government tenders for projects should comply. Many will follow.

3 Summary of the method

ISO 21500 provides guidance for project management and can be used by any type of organization, including public, private or community organizations, and for any type of project, irrespective of complexity, size or duration. ISO 21500 provides high-level description of concepts and processes that are considered to form good practice in project management. Projects are placed in the context of programmes and project portfolios, however, ISO 21500 does not provide detailed guidance on the management of programmes and project portfolios. Topics pertaining to general management are addressed only within the context of project management. (Source: www.iso.org)

ISO 21500 is a publication of the International Organization for Standardization, the world's largest developer of voluntary International Standards, to provide good practice in project management, helping to make industry more efficient and effective. During the five years it took to complete, ISO 21500 was developed on the basis of inputs from hundreds of project management experts, standards development committees from more than thirty countries and project management associations like IPMA (International Project Management Association) and PMI (Project Management Institute). It was published in September 2012.

ISO 21500 is the first of a family of ISO standards for the portfolio, programme and project management landscape, currently under development. This will be based on an overall framework that defines project, programme and portfolio management (PPP), including the governance and terminology. Also it will define the interaction between PPP processes and the organization they serve, including the governance dimension and the links to ongoing operations. Projects may be organized within programme and project portfolios.

ISO 21500 is process-based: it describes work as being accomplished by processes. This approach is consistent with other management standards such as ISO/IEC 9001:2008 and the Software Engineering Institute's CMMI. Processes overlap and interact throughout a project or its various phases. Processes are described in terms of purpose, description and primary inputs (documents, plans, designs, etc.), and outputs (documents, products, etc.).

The guideline identifies 39 processes that fall into five basic process groups and ten subject groups that cover the typical managerial aspects for almost every project.

The five process groups are Initiating, Planning, Implementing, Controlling and Closing.
The ten subject groups are Integration, Stakeholder, Scope, Resource, Time, Cost, Risk, Quality, Procurement and Communication.

Each of the ten subject groups contains the processes that need to be accomplished within its discipline in order to achieve effective management of a project. Each of these processes also falls into one of the five basic process groups, creating a matrix structure such that every process can be related to one subject group and one process group.

4   Target audience

All roles with an interest in project management, such as senior managers and project sponsors, project managers, project management teams, and project team members, but also members of a project office, customers and other project stakeholders. It may be used by any type of organization (public, private, community organizations, ..) and for all types of project, with different levels of complexity, size, or duration.

5   Scope and constraints

ISO 21500 is a generic approach that can be applied to any project.

Strengths
- Extensive participation by different industry sectors and organizations that are using project management and developing project management good practices all over the world
- Recognized as a 'globally accepted' standard in the profession
- Generic; it can be applied to any project
- Focus on process, similar to other frameworks and standards from ISO

Constraints
- ISO 21500 is high-level and generic and therefore not exhaustive
- It does not provide real life examples, methods and tools and techniques.

6　Relevant website

www.iso.org

ISO 31000

1 Title/current version

ISO 31000:2009 Standard for Risk Management

2 The basics

ISO 31000:2009 comprises principles, a framework and a process for the management of risk that is applicable to any type of organization in the public or private sector.

3 Summary

ISO 31000:2009 provides guidance on the implementation of risk management. It was first published as a standard in November 2009, and is owned by the International Standards Organization (ISO). The ISO 31000 family includes:

- ISO 31000:2009 – Principles and Guidelines on Implementation
- ISO/IEC 31010:2009 – Risk Management – Risk Assessment Techniques
- ISO Guide 73:2009 – Risk Management – Vocabulary

ISO 31000 provides generic guidelines for the design, implementation and maintenance of risk management processes throughout an organization. The scope of this approach to risk management is to enable all strategic, management and operational tasks of an organization throughout projects, functions, and processes to be aligned to a common set of risk management objectives.

ISO 31000:2009 comprises three building blocks (see Figure).

The First Building Block, the Risk Management Infrastructure, states that risk management should contain the following principles:

- Creates value
- Integral part of organizational processes
- Part of decision-making
- Explicitly addresses uncertainty
- Systematic, structured and timely
- Based on the best available information
- Tailored to the organization
- Takes human and cultural factors into account
- Transparent and inclusive
- Dynamic, iterative and responsive to change
- Facilitates continual improvement of the organization

The Second Building Block, the Risk Management Framework, is about creating the right risk framework through management commitment. Once commitment is established, there is a cycle of actions that include the following steps:

1. Design
2. Implementation
3. Monitoring and review
4. Continual improvement

The Third Building Block, the Risk Management Process, was originally adopted from the standard AS/NZS 4360:2004, which assures that communication and monitoring is done throughout the process.

4 Target audience

Business managers, risk management officers, CIOs, information security officers.

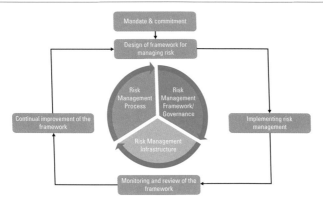

Figure: Building blocks of ISO 31000:2009

5 Scope and constraints

ISO 31000:2009 can be applied throughout the life of an organization, and to a wide range of activities, including strategies and decisions, operations, processes, functions, projects, products, services and assets. It can be applied to any type of risk, whatever its nature, whether having positive or negative consequences.

ISO 31000:2009 is a concise standard that reflects current international thinking. This is a very positive development in the risk management standards landscape. However, a constraint might be that it still has to prove itself. At the present date, there are not many actual implementations in organizations.

6 Relevant website

www.iso.org

MoP™

1 Title/current version

MoP™ (Management of Portfolios)

2 The basics

MoP™ is a framework for understanding, prioritizing and planning a portfolio of business change initiatives; it is a coordinated collection of strategic processes and decisions that together enable the most effective balance of organizational change and 'business as usual'.

3 Summary

The MoP guide was published by the Cabinet Office in 2011. The guide addresses the question of what changes, programmes and projects should be undertaken by an organization today and tomorrow, and those it should support in the future. Its primary aim is to support those with strategic or change portfolio responsibility to make appropriate change investment decisions in a logical, transparent and efficient way.

Portfolio management is not concerned with the detailed management of the projects and programmes: rather, it approaches the management of change projects and programmes from a strategic viewpoint.

MoP addresses the challenges of *'Run the Business vs. Change the Business'*. Organizations expend energy on running their operations well. Most organizations also adopt and embed consistent programme, project and change management methods. MoP provides the interface between these elements.

Portfolio management aims to address the following fundamental questions:

- Are we doing the right things?
- Are we doing these things right?
- Most significantly, are we realizing all the benefits in terms of more effective services and efficiency savings from the changes we are implementing?

The mechanisms by which these questions are answered are incorporated in the MoP framework (see Figure). This framework brings together the key activities required to successfully define and deliver a portfolio of change whilst ensuring resources are used efficiently.

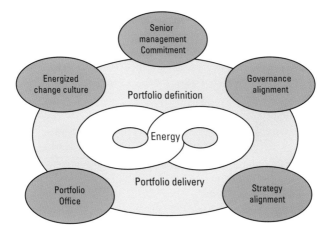

Figure: MoP framework
Source: AXELOS

This framework consists of two portfolio management cycles, portfolio definition and portfolio delivery, and of five portfolio management principles:

- Senior management commitment
- Governance alignment
- Strategy alignment
- Portfolio Office
- Energized change culture

4 Target audience

Senior management, people responsible for governance and all those with strategic or change portfolio responsibility.

5 Scope and constraints

The scope of the method comprises the different decision – making processes around strategic change initiatives within organizations. MoP is part of the Best Management Practice methods developed by the Cabinet Office. This means that it is fully aligned with PRINCE2®, MSP® and P3O®.

The MoP guidance claims that it helps organizations to understand which change initiatives contribute most to their strategy and enables them to make informed decisions about their overall status, prioritization, risk and benefits.

6 Relevant website

www.axelos.com

M_o_R®

1 Title/current version
M_o_R® (Management of Risk) 2010 Edition

2 The basics
Management of Risk, M_o_R is a structured framework and
process for taking informed decisions about the risks that affect
an organization, at a strategic, programme, project or operational
level.

3 Summary
M_o_R® was first published in 2002; its current version is the
2010 Edition. The approach was originally designed for use by
the UK Government and is now owned by AXELOS. It is used in
the public and private sectors alike.

Management of Risk is of enterprise-wide importance, and can
be applied to the three core elements of a business (see Figure):
- Strategic – business direction
- Change – turning strategy into action, including programme,
  project and change management
- Operational – day-to-day operation and support of the business

In this way, the strategy for managing risk should be managed
from the top of the organization while being embedded into the
normal working routines and activities of the organization.

There are eight principles, which are consistent with corporate
governance principles and the international standard for risk
management ISO 31000: 2009. The principles are: Aligns with

objectives; Fits the context; Engages stakeholders; Provides clear guidance; Informs decision-making; Facilitates continual improvement; Creates a supportive culture; Achieves measurable value.

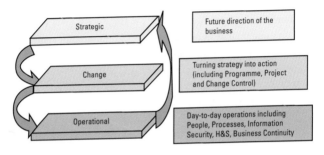

Figure: The three core elements of business where M_o_R can be applied
Source: AXELOS

An overall strategic framework, including a policy document, is also of key importance. It needs to include the following elements: risk identification; risk evaluation; setting acceptable levels of risk; identifying suitable responses to risks; risk ownership; implementing responses to risks; gaining assurance about the effectiveness of the responses; embedding, reporting and review.

Once a framework is in place, a common approach can be used across the business, bringing together disparate risk disciplines and functions into a consolidated and consistent approach.

4 Target audience

Business managers, risk management officers, CIOs, information security officers; programme and project managers.

5 Scope and constraints

M_o_R is appropriate for any type of organization regardless of its size, complexity, location, or sector.

Strengths
- Improved corporate decision-making through the effective communication of risk exposure throughout the organization
- An open and supportive approach to the identification, analysis and communication of risk
- Better awareness in all personnel of the cost and benefit implications of their actions

Constraints
In practice, it is often difficult to ensure that all risk-related disciplines and resulting work are captured within a consolidated view of risk, as there can be a tendency to work in segregated functional areas – especially in larger organizations.

6 Relevant website

www.axelos.com

MoV

1 Title/current version
Management of Value (MoV)

2 The basics:
MoV helps to:
- Deliver more of the right things
- Reduce the cost of delivery
- Encourage more effective use of available resources

3 Summary
MoV was first published in 2010 and answers the question: are we getting the optimal benefits, at affordable costs, with an acceptable risk level? The Figure shows that we have to achieve the optimal balance between all stakeholders' needs, and the usage of resources (money, people, time, energy and material). The greater the benefits delivered and the fewer resources that are used in doing so, the higher the value ratio.

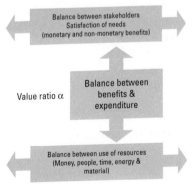

Figure: Balancing the variables to maximize value

MoV is based on four integrated concepts:

1. Principles (factors that underpin MoV).
2. Processes and techniques: methods and tools used in the application of MoV.
3. Approach: how to apply MoV in running your business and changing your business.
4. Environment: how to respond to internal and external influences.

The seven principles represent the most important factors in delivering success. The seven principles are:

1. Align with organizational objectives.
2. Focus on functions and required outcomes. Start with the end in mind. What benefits and outcomes do you need?
3. Balance the variables to maximize value. Understand the key stakeholder needs and balance these needs to make them acceptable to everybody. Balance these needs against the use of resources like money, people, time, energy and material.
4. Apply throughout the investment decision. MoV is applied during all stages of the change lifecycle.
5. Tailor to suit the subject. The complexity, size, culture, involved risks, etc. will impact the level of effort needed to apply MoV.
6. Learn from experience. Do not re-invent the wheel, don't stumble twice over one stone. Share, share, and share your lessons learned.
7. Assign clear roles and responsibilities and build a supportive culture. If there is no senior management buy-in and there are no clearly assigned roles and responsibilities it will be a guarantee for failure.

MoV is achieved in programmes and projects through seven main (groups of) processes. The seven processes are:

1. Frame the programme or project. Understand the rationale behind the project or programme and the objectives to be achieved.
2. Gather information. What are the expectations from the MoV study, who do we need on the MoV team, who are the stakeholders, what are their needs?
3. Analyze information. Enrich the gathered information, use techniques like FAST (see below) to understand the purpose and analyze alternative ways of performing or delivering the functions.
4. Process information. The MoV team will use the information to explore alternatives and create innovative and value-adding proposals. This could also mean that specific functions that are not needed will be eliminated (compare the MoSCoW principle in an Agile approach).
5. Evaluate and select. Here we balance the variables (stakeholder needs, required resources, benefits at affordable costs) to maximize the value.
6. Develop value-improving proposals.
7. Implement and share outputs. Develop the plan, implement, monitor progress and gather lessons learned and share.

MoV uses MoV-specific and common techniques such as Function Analysis System Technique (FAST), Value trees, Function Cost Analysis and Value Engineering (VE).

4 Target audience
PPM community, senior managers and risk (opportunities) and operational managers.

5 Scope and constraints

The scope of MoV is intended for operational activities as well as programmes and projects.

Strengths

- Embedding the mindset of thinking 'value' and reducing waste
- Increased stakeholder commitment
- More effective use of resources
- Better control over delivery. Projects that do not add value are cancelled or not started
- Greater responsiveness to a changing environment
- Improvements in return on investments

Constraints / MoV barriers:

- We are already doing okay without it
- I haven't got the time or the money to spare for this
- There is no benefit for me

6 Relevant website

www.axelos.com

MSP®

1 Title/current version

MSP® (Managing Successful Programmes) 2011 Edition

2 The basics

MSP® (Managing Successful Programmes) is a systematic approach to managing programmes of business change to achieve outcomes and realize benefits that are of strategic importance.

3 Summary of the method

MSP® (Managing Successful Programmes) was first published in 1999 by the UK Office of Government Commerce (OGC). It is now owned by AXELOS. The current version is MSP 2011 Edition.

MSP describes best practice for managing programmes of business change. Within MSP a programme is defined as a portfolio of projects and (business) activities that are coordinated and managed as units. The goal is to achieve outcomes and realize benefits that are of strategic importance.

The MSP framework is based on three core concepts (see Figure): principles, governance themes and transformational flow.

- MSP principles (outer ring); these are derived from lessons learned in programmes with both positive and negative results. They represent common factors that underpin the success of any programmes of transformational change
- MSP governance themes (middle ring); these themes show how an organization's approach to programme management needs to be defined, measured and controlled. The gover-

nance themes allow organizations to put in place the appropriate leadership, delivery team, robust organization structures, controls and control information (e.g. blueprint, business case, quality and assurance strategy), giving the best chance of delivering the planned outcomes and realizing the desired benefits

- MSP transformational flow (inner circle); this flow provides a route through the lifecycle of a programme from its conception through to delivering the new capability, transitioning to the desired outcomes, realizing the benefits and finally closing the programmes.

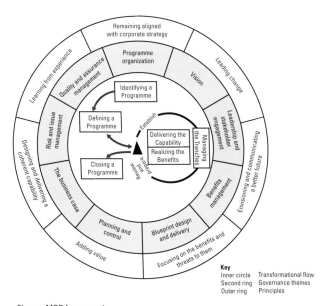

Figure: MSP framework
Source: AXELOS

4 Target audience

The main target audience is senior executives, programme managers and business change managers. However, all roles involved in business change (such as business and functional managers and other stakeholders) may find it useful to understand the principles of programme management.

5 Scope and constraints

The scope of the method comprises all the processes and activities within the programme management lifecycle.

Strengths

MSP is a best practice method in programme management with:
- A focus on achieving outcomes and realizing benefits
- A good description of the characteristics and concepts of programme management
- A focus on added value and management of risks
- Clear terms of reference for all roles within the programme management structure
- A focus on processes: it describes all processes and activities within the processes of programme management
- Outlines for all programme management products

MSP can be seamlessly combined with the PRINCE2® project management approach. They have the same owner: AXELOS and they contain a similar process-based management approach.

6 Relevant website

www.axelos.com

P3M3®

1 Title/current version

P3M3® Portfolio, Programme, and Project Management Maturity Model.

2 The basics

P3M3® has become a key standard amongst maturity models, providing a framework with which organizations can assess their current performance and put improvement plans in place.

3 Summary

P3M3® was released in June 2008, with a further update, Version 2.1, being released in February 2010. The first version was developed as an enhancement to OGC's Project Management Maturity Model. P3M3® is now owned by AXELOS.

P3M3® consists of a hierarchical collection of elements describing the characteristics of effective processes.

Maturity Levels
P3M3® uses a five-level maturity framework:
- Level 1 – awareness of process
- Level 2 – repeatable process
- Level 3 – defined process
- Level 4 – managed process
- Level 5 – optimized process

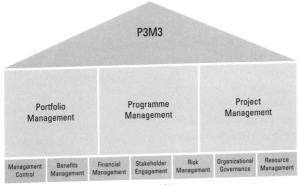

Figure: P3M3®, the model (*source:* AXELOS)

Process Perspectives

P3M3® focuses on seven Process Perspectives, which exist in all three models and can be assessed at all five Maturity Levels:

1. Management Control
2. Benefits Management
3. Financial Management
4. Stakeholder Engagement
5. Risk Management
6. Organizational Governance
7. Resource Management

Attributes

Embedded within the Process Perspectives are a number of Attributes. Specific Attributes relate only to a particular Process Perspective. Generic Attributes are common to all Process

Perspectives at a given Maturity Level, and include planning, information management, and training and development.

4 Target audience

The main target audience is senior executives, portfolio managers and programme managers. However, all roles involved in the maturity of portfolio, programme and project management may find it useful to gain a better understanding of their strengths and weaknesses in order to enable improvement to happen.

5 Scope

P3M3® is a maturity assessment model to assess the project management and programme management as well as the portfolio management in an organization. P3M3® is not an assessment tool for individual projects or programmes.

Strengths

As organizations strive to identify competitive and performance advantages, and leverage them through improved efficiency and delivery, management models designed to assess performance and identify opportunities for improvement are increasingly important. Maturity models in particular have become an essential tool in assessing organizations' current capabilities and helping them to implement change and improvements in a structured way.

The flexibility of P3M3® allows organizations to review all seven Process Perspectives across all three models – portfolio, programme and project management – but they can also review

project management

just one (or several) of the Process Perspectives, whether across all three models or across only one or two of them. This can be useful to gain a better understanding of an organization's overall effectiveness in, for example, risk management or resource management.

6 Relevant website

www.axelos.com

P3O®

1 Title/current version
P3O® (Portfolio, Programme and Project Offices)

2 The basics
P3O® (Portfolio, Programme and Project Offices) is a decision enabling/delivery-support model for all business change within an organization, typically providing support through a Portfolio Office, a Programme Management Office, a Project Support Office or any combination of these delivery support functions.

3 Summary
P3O (Portfolio, Programme and Project Offices) was first published in 2008 and is now owned by AXELOS.

P3O offers guidance for setting up and running support offices, for all levels of change within an organization. It offers advice to organizations on current best practice thinking about what previously was referred to as PSO (Programme or Project Support Office) or PMO (Programme or Project Management Office).

The main functions of a P3O/ PMO in an organization are to facilitate:
- Informing senior management's decision-making on prioritization, risk management and development of resources across the organization to successfully deliver their business objectives (portfolio management)
- Identification and realization of outcomes and benefits through programmes and projects

- Delivery of programmes and projects within time, cost, quality and other organizational constraints

As a decision-enabling/delivery support model, P3O may be a single permanent office, e.g. Portfolio Office (strategically focused), a Strategy or Business Planning Unit, a Centre of Excellence, or an Enterprise/Corporate Programme Office. It may also be a linked set of offices e.g. Portfolio Office, Programme Offices and Project Offices; or it may be a permanent or temporary mix of central and localized services.

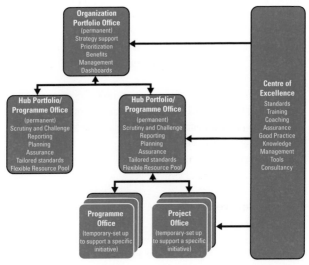

Figure: P3O model for large organizations
Source: AXELOS

4 Target audience

Portfolio managers, senior managers, programme directors, consultants, portfolio-, programme- or project office managers who are involved in, or responsible for, optimizing, developing or re-energizing the organizational decision process to translate business strategy effectively into concrete actions, programmes or projects.

5 Scope and constraints

The scope of the method is the support structures and processes around strategic change initiatives and their delivery via programmes and projects within organizations.

P3O is part of the Best Management Practice methods owned by AXELOS. This means it is fully aligned with PRINCE2®, MSP® and MoP®.

The P3O guidance claims that the method can significantly increase an organization's chances of successfully delivering its strategy, reducing the number of benefits not delivered and delivering programmes and projects more cost effectively. The approach is fairly new and not yet widely adopted.

6 Relevant website

www.axelos.com

PMBOK® Guide

1 Title/current version

A Guide to the Project Management Body of Knowledge
(*PMBOK® Guide*) 5th Edition

2 The basics

*A Guide to the Project Management Body of Knowledge
(PMBOK® Guide)* is a guide providing a comprehensive set
of knowledge, concepts, techniques and skills for the project
management profession.

3 Summary of the method

The *PMBOK® Guide* is a publication from the Project Management
Institute (PMI), an entity that is globally recognized as governing
the project management discipline. PMI was founded in 1969 in
the US and has become one of the principal professional non-profit
organizations in the specialism. The first edition of the guide was
published in 1996; the latest English-language *PMBOK® Guide* -
Fifth Edition, was released in January 2013.

The *PMBOK® Guide* is process-based: it describes work as being
accomplished by processes. This approach is consistent with other
management standards such as ISO 21500 for Project Management,
ISO/IEC 9001:2008 and the Software Engineering Institute's
CMMI. Processes overlap and interact throughout a project or
its various phases. Processes are described in terms of inputs
(documents, plans, designs, etc.), tools and techniques (mechanisms
applied to inputs) and outputs (documents, products, etc.)

The guide identifies 47 processes that fall into five basic process groups
and ten knowledge areas that are typical for almost every project.

The five process groups are Initiating, Planning, Executing, Monitoring and Controlling, and Closing.

The ten knowledge areas are Project Integration Management, Project Scope Management, Project Time Management, Project Cost Management, Project Quality Management, Project Human Resource Management, Project Communications Management, Project Risk Management, Project Procurement Management and Stakeholder Management.

Each of the ten knowledge areas contains the processes that are advised to be accomplished within its discipline in order to achieve effective management of a project. Each of these processes also falls into one of the five basic process groups, creating a matrix structure such that every process can be related to one knowledge area and one process group.

4 Target audience

Although the publication typically targets (senior) project managers, the processes described involve all roles with an interest in project management, such as senior executives, programme and project managers, project team members, members of a project office, customers and other stakeholders, consultants and other specialists. As an introduction, an easy accessible pocket publication is also available, aimed at a broader audience involved in projects.

5 Scope and constraints

PMBOK® Guide is a generic approach that can be applied to any project.

Strengths

- Extensive participation by different industry sectors and organizations that are using project management all over the world
- Recognized as a 'world class' standard in the profession and, because of that, used as the book of reference for many other project management standards and methods
- Generic; it can be applied to any project
- Focus on process, similar to other frameworks and standards in use such as ITIL®, COBIT® and ISO*. Fully aligned to the latest global project management standard, ISO 21500
- Evolution and continuous improvement in line with modern concepts of quality
- Certification programmes (PMP and CAPM) associated and guaranteed deployment of accreditation skills from all over the world.* Fully aligned with the broader concept of project, programme and portfolio management (PMI provides additional standards for this)

Constraints

- The *PMBOK® Guide* is not exhaustive: although the *PMBOK® Guide* provides tools and techniques for the application of processes, it does not provide a method.
- The *PMBOK® Guide* does not provide real life examples of tools and templates for practical application
- The *PMBOK® Guide* is more of a framework a (conceptual over-arching and generic model) than a method (for direct practical application)

6 Relevant website

www.pmi.org/

Praxis Framework™

1 Title/definition
The Praxis Framework. First released in May 2014.

2 The basics
Praxis is the first best practice framework to integrate projects, programmes and portfolios in a single guide and is also the first to be made available free of charge on the World Wide Web. It contains five main sections: a body of knowledge; a methodology, a competency framework, a capability maturity model and an encyclopaedia of tools and techniques.

Praxis is the first guide to fully integrate these five areas so that organisations do not have to incur the costs of integrating multiple guides that use different taxonomies and variable terminologies.

For organizational implementation of project, programme and portfolio management (P3M), Praxis provides additional resources, including a free 360° capability maturity assessment tool, a comparative glossary for translating between all the major guides, templates, free on-line books and an indexed portal to additional free content on the web.

3 Summary
Praxis integrates knowledge and method to provide life cycle processes and the functions needed to implement them. Its complementary competency framework and capability maturity model ensure that both knowledge and method are applied at both the individual and organisational level.

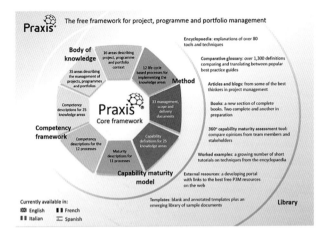

By making the framework freely available on the World Wide Web, Praxis is demystifying the P3M discipline and detaching it from heavily copyrighted brands and their corporate marketing. Every page on the web site has a comments feature and a 'contact us' tab that enables all practitioners to contribute to the evolution of the framework.

The structure of Praxis will be familiar to users of existing guides. The knowledge section adheres to the format and principles of the APM Body of Knowledge, the process model combines the principles of PRINCE2® and MSP® into a single approach to project and programmes, and the capability maturity model is based on CMMI-Dev. The difference is Praxis applies all these principles using a single taxonomy and terminology.

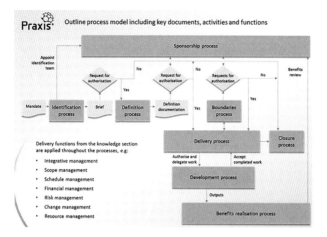

The inherent flexibility of the framework also allows other
models to be introduced, such as the ISO21500 life cycle
processes that are very similar to the PMBoK® Guide from PMI®.

4 Target audience

Project managers, programme managers, portfolio managers,
PMO managers, sponsors, team members and senior
management involved in decision-making activities in the P3M
environment.

5 Strengths

Praxis is generic and flexible so that it can be used in any
industry, organization, geography or culture.

By bringing the five sections of a successful P3M implementation
together in a single framework, it greatly reduces the time
required to set up consistent and robust organisational practices.

The integral 360° capability maturity process ensures that improvement starts on day one by supporting project and programme managers in their day-to-day implementation of best practice principles.

Praxis is not a static source of information. Industry experts regularly contribute additional material that is cross referenced within the framework. Links to curated free content from around the web are regularly updated.

The framework can easily be tailored and in one example, the web site provides an explanation of how to use Praxis to support an ISO21500 compatible implementation.

Languages

Praxis is currently available in English, French, Spanish and Italian. Chinese is in preparation and other languages will follow.

6 Relevant websites

www.praxisframework.org
https://www.apm.org.uk/book-shop/praxis-framework/

Praxis Framework™ is a trademark of Praxis Framework Limited.
PRINCE2® and MSP® are registered trademarks of AXELOS Limited. PMBOK® is a registered trademark of PMI®.

PRINCE2®-2017 Edition

1 Title/current version

Managing Successful Projects with PRINCE2® (PRojects IN Controlled environments) First released in 1989 as PRINCE and renamed PRINCE2 when revised in 1996, further revisions in 2005, 2009, 2017. PRINCE2 is now owned by AXELOS.

2 The basics

PRINCE2 is one of the most widely used methods for managing projects in the world. It is a structured and process based project management method. PRINCE2 provides a tried and tested method based on experience from which all projects and organizations can benefit.

This latest evolution of PRINCE2-2017 will help understand how the fundamental principles of PRINCE2 provide the basis of good project management. It emphasizes how the method can be tailored to give an appropriate fit to projects. It offers practical guidance on managing projects within many contexts including those using agile approaches.

3 Summary

PRINCE2 has been designed to be generic so that it can be applied to any project regardless of project scale, type, organization, geography or culture. It achieves this by separating the management of project work from the specialist contributions, such as design or construction. These specialist aspects of any type of project are easily integrated and/or used alongside PRINCE2. It provides a secure overall framework for the project work focusing on describing *WHAT* needs to be done, rather than prescribing *HOW* everything is done.

For a project to be following PRINCE2, as a minimum it must be possible to demonstrate that the project:

- is applying principles of PRINCE2 (continued business justification, learn from experience, defined roles and responsibilities, manage by stages, manage by exception, focus on products, tailor to suit the project.
- is meeting the minimum requirements set out in the PRINCE2 themes (Business Case, Organization, Quality, Plan, Risk, Change and Progress)
- has project processes that satisfy the purpose and objectives of the PRINCE2 processes
- is either using PRINCE2's recommended techniques e.g. Quality Review or using alternative, equivalent techniques

PRINCE2 is based on proven experience and governance for project management and must be tailored to the specific context of a project. The needs of the organization and scaled to the size and complexity of a project. It provides a common language (a 'PM-dialect') for all project participants to facilitate communication and promotes consistency of project work and the ability to reuse project assets. This also facilitates staff mobility and reduces the impact of personnel changes or handovers. Furthermore, it ensures that participants focus on the viability of the project in relation to its business case objectives, rather than simply seeing the completion of the project as an end in itself. PRINCE2 ensures that stakeholders (including sponsors and resource providers) are properly represented in decision-making and planning. And last but not least it promotes learning from project experience and continual improvement in organizations

PRINCE2 provides a process model for managing a project (see Figure). These processes consist of a set of activities that are required to direct, manage and deliver a project.

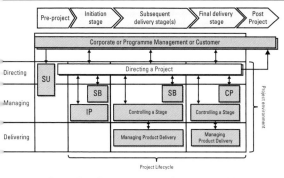

Figure: PRINCE2 process model (*Source:* AXELOS)

4 Target audience

Project managers, project team members, senior management involved in the decision-making activities of the project.

5 Scope and constraints

PRINCE2 is generic so that can be used for any project regardless of project scale, type, organization, geography or culture.

Constraints: PRINCE2 is not intended to cover every aspect of Project Management. It does not contain topics such as:

Specialist aspects: PRINCE2 is generic and excludes industry/type-specific activity. Engineering models, agile methods or specific techniques (e.g. organizational change management, procurement, SCRUM can be used alongside PRINCE2)

Detailed techniques: Proven planning and control techniques that can be used in support of the PRINCE2 themes; for example, critical path analysis (in planning) and Earned Value Analysis (in progress control).

Leadership capability: Leadership, motivational skills and other

interpersonal and soft skills are critical success factors in project management but impossible to codify in a method

6 Relevant website

www.axelos.com

enterprise architecture

ArchiMate®

1 Title/current version
ArchiMate® 2.1, an Open Group Standard

2 The basics
ArchiMate® is an open and independent modeling language for Enterprise Architecture that is supported by different tool vendors and consulting firms. ArchiMate provides instruments to enable enterprise architects to describe, analyze, and visualize the relationships between business domains in an unambiguous way.

3 Summary
Developed by the members of The Open Group, ArchiMate® 2.1 was released in December 2013 and is aligned with TOGAF®, the world's most popular Enterprise Architecture framework. As a result, enterprise architects using the language can improve the way key business and IT stakeholders collaborate and adapt to change.

The standard contains the formal definition of ArchiMate as a visual design language, together with concepts for specifying inter-related architectures, and specific viewpoints for typical stakeholders. The standard also includes a chapter addressing considerations regarding language extensions.

The contents of the standard include the following:
- The overall modeling framework that ArchiMate uses
- The structure of the modeling language

- A detailed breakdown of the constituent elements of the modeling framework covering the three layers (Business/Application/Technology), cross-layer dependencies and alignment, and relationships within the framework
- Architectural viewpoints, including a set of standard viewpoints
- Optional extensions to the framework
- Commentary around future direction of the specification
- Notation overviews and summaries

ArchiMate 2.1 improves collaboration through clearer understanding across multiple functions, including business executives, enterprise architects, systems analysts, software engineers, business process consultants, and infrastructure engineers. The standard enables the creation of fully integrated models of an organization's Enterprise Architecture, the motivation behind it, and the programmes, projects, and migration paths to implement it. ArchiMate already follows terms defined in the TOGAF framework, and Version 2.1 of the specification enables modeling throughout the TOGAF Architecture Development Method (ADM) cycle.

4 Target audience

Enterprise architects, business architects, IT architects, application architects, data architects, software architects, systems architects, solutions architects, infrastructure architects, process architects, domain architects, product managers, operational managers, senior managers, project leaders, and anyone committed to working within the reference framework defined by an Enterprise Architecture.

5 Scope

The role of the ArchiMate standard is to provide a graphical
language for the representation of Enterprise Architectures over
time (i.e., including transformation and migration planning),
as well as their motivation and rationale. The ArchiMate
modeling language provides a uniform representation for
diagrams that describe Enterprise Architectures, and offers
an integrated approach to describe and visualize the different
architecture domains together with their underlying relations and
dependencies.

The design of the ArchiMate language started from a set of
relatively generic concepts (objects and relations), which have
been specialized for application at the different architectural
layers for an Enterprise Architecture. The most important design
restriction on ArchiMate is that it has been explicitly designed
to be as compact as possible, yet still usable for most Enterprise
Architecture modeling tasks. In the interest of simplicity of
learning and use, ArchiMate has been limited to the concepts
that suffice for modeling the proverbial 80% of practical cases.

6 Relevant website

www.opengroup.org/archimate

IT4IT™

1 Title/Current Version

IT4IT™ Reference Architecture Version 2.1, an Open Group Standard.

2 The Basics

The Open Group IT4IT Reference Architecture is a standard reference architecture for managing the business of IT. It uses a value chain approach to create a model of the functions that IT performs to help organizations identify the activities that contribute to business competitiveness.

The IT Value Chain

The IT Value Chain has four value streams supported by a reference architecture to drive efficiency and agility. The four value streams are:

- Strategy to Portfolio
- Request to Fulfill
- Requirement to Deploy
- Detect to Correct

Each IT Value Stream is centered on a key aspect of the service model, the essential data objects (information model), and functional components (functional model) that support it. Together, the four value streams play a vital role in helping IT control the service model as it advances through its lifecycle.

The IT4IT Reference Architecture Standard:

- Provides a vendor-neutral, technology-agnostic, and industry-agnostic reference architecture for managing the business of IT, enabling insight for continuous improvement.

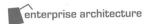

- Provides the capabilities for managing the business of IT that will enable IT execution across the entire Value Chain in a better, faster, cheaper way with less risk.
- Provides prescriptive guidance on the specification of and interaction with a consistent service model backbone (common data model/context)
- Supports real-world use-cases driven by the Digital Economy (e.g., Cloud-sourcing, Agile, DevOps, and service brokering)
- Embraces and complements existing process frameworks and methodologies (e.g., ITIL®, CoBIT®, SAFe, and TOGAF®) by taking a data-focused implementation model perspective, essentially specifying an information model across the entire value chain
- Is industry-independent to solve the same problems for everyone.
- Is designed for existing landscapes and accommodates future IT paradigms.

3 Summary

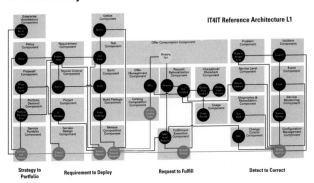

The IT4IT Reference Architecture standard consists of the IT value chain and a three-layer reference architecture. Level 1 is shown below.

The IT4IT Reference Architecture provides prescriptive, holistic guidance for the implementation of IT management capabilities for today's digital enterprise. It is positioned as a peer to comparable reference architectures such as NRF/ARTS, TMF Framework (aka eTOM), ACORD, BIAN, and other such guidance.

Together, the four value streams play a vital role in helping IT control the service model as it advances through its lifecycle:

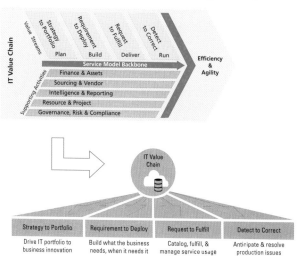

The **Strategy to Portfolio** (S2P) Value Stream:
- Provides the strategy to balance and broker your portfolio
- Provides a unified viewpoint across PMO, enterprise architecture, and service portfolio

- Improves data quality for decision-making
- Provides KPIs and roadmaps to improve business communication

The **Requirement to Deploy** (R2D) Value Stream:
- Provides a framework for creating, modifying, or sourcing a service
- Supports agile and traditional development methodologies
- Enables visibility of the quality, utility, schedule, and cost of the services you deliver
- Defines continuous integration and deployment control points

The **Request to Fulfill** (R2F) Value Stream:
- Helps your IT organization transition to a service broker model
- Presents a single catalog with items from multiple supplier catalogs
- Efficiently manages subscriptions and total cost of service
- Manages and measures fulfillments across multiple suppliers

The **Detect to Correct** (D2C) Value Stream:
- Brings together IT service operations to enhance results and efficiency
- Enables end-to-end visibility using a shared configuration model
- Identifies issues before they affect users
- Reduces the mean time to repair

Version 2.1 Release Highlights
The following topics have been included/enhanced in Version 2.1 of the IT4IT Reference Architecture:

- Service Model simplification and enhancement – The data objects which make up the Service Model Backbone have been simplified and better defined to lead to a stronger understanding of the Reference Architecture in its entirety. The Service Model is the backbone of the entire standard.
- Financial Management supporting function – The Reference Architecture has been updated to highlight how financial management capabilities are now supported by the standard. Financial Management is one of the Supporting Functions in the overall IT Value Chain and has impacts on core functions and data objects which have been updated to more effectively support this capability.
- General consistency and flow of the overall standard – The Reference Architecture 2.0 was the first version of the standard which was published. There were certain sections, naming conventions, and content which lacked some consistency throughout the standard which have now been resolved.

4 Target Audience

The target audience for the standard consists of:
- IT executives
- IT process analysts
- Architects tasked with "business of IT" questions
- Development and operations managers
- Consultants and trainers active in the IT industry

5 Scope

The Open Group IT4IT standard is focused on defining, sourcing, consuming, and managing IT services by looking holistically at the entire IT Value Chain. While existing frameworks and standards have placed their main emphasis on

process, this standard is process-agnostic, focused instead on the data needed to manage a service through its lifecycle. It then describes the functional components (software) that are required to produce and consume the data. Once integrated together, a system of record fabric for IT management is created that ensures full visibility and traceability of the service from cradle to grave.

IT4IT is neutral with respect to development and delivery models. It is intended to support Agile as well as waterfall approaches, and lean Kanban process approaches as well as fully elaborated IT service management process models.

The IT4IT Reference Architecture relates to TOGAF, ArchiMate, and ITIL as shown below:

6 Relevant Website

www.opengroup.org/IT4IT

TOGAF®

1 Title/current version

TOGAF® Version 9.1, an Open Group Standard

2 The basics

TOGAF® – the Enterprise Architecture standard used by the world's leading organizations to improve business efficiency.

3 Summary

TOGAF®, is a proven Enterprise Architecture methodology and framework used by the world's leading organizations to improve business efficiency. It is the most prominent and reliable Enterprise Architecture standard, ensuring consistent standards, methods, and communication among Enterprise Architecture professionals. Enterprise Architecture professionals fluent in TOGAF standards enjoy greater industry credibility, job effectiveness, and career opportunities. TOGAF helps practitioners avoid being locked into proprietary methods, utilize resources more efficiently and effectively, and realize a greater return on investment.

TOGAF has been continuously evolved and improved by the members of The Open Group since it was first published by them in 1995. The Open Group is a global consortium that enables the achievement of business objectives through IT standards. With more than 400 member organizations, the diverse membership spans all sectors of the IT community — customers, systems and solutions suppliers, tool vendors, integrators and consultants, as well as academics and researchers.

TOGAF Version 9.1 is a maintenance update to TOGAF 9, addressing comments raised since the introduction of TOGAF 9 in 2009. It retains the major features and structure of TOGAF 9, thereby preserving existing investment in TOGAF, and adds further detail and clarification to what is already proven.

The standard is divided into seven parts:

- PART I (Introduction): This part provides a high-level introduction to the key concepts of Enterprise Architecture and in particular the TOGAF approach. It contains the definitions of terms used throughout TOGAF and release notes detailing the changes between this version and the previous version of TOGAF

- PART II (Architecture Development Method): This is the core of TOGAF. It describes the TOGAF Architecture Development Method (ADM) – a step-by-step approach to developing an Enterprise Architecture

- PART III (ADM Guidelines & Techniques): This part contains a collection of guidelines and techniques available for use in applying TOGAF and the TOGAF ADM

- PART IV (Architecture Content Framework): This part describes the TOGAF content framework, including a structured metamodel for architectural artifacts, the use of re-usable architecture building blocks, and an overview of typical architecture deliverables

- PART V (Enterprise Continuum & Tools): This part discusses appropriate taxonomies and tools to categorize and store the outputs of architecture activity within an enterprise

- PART VI (TOGAF Reference Models): This part provides a selection of architectural reference models, which includes the TOGAF Foundation Architecture and the Integrated Information Infrastructure Reference Model (III-RM)

- PART VII (Architecture Capability Framework): This part discusses the organization, processes, skills, roles, and responsibilities required to establish and operate an architecture function within an enterprise

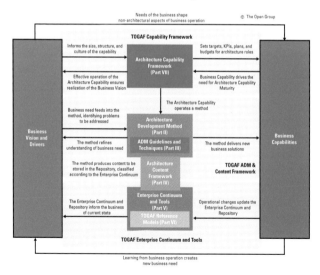

Figure: Components of TOGAF
Source: The Open Group

Central to TOGAF is the Architecture Development Method (documented in TOGAF, Part II). The architecture capability (documented in TOGAF, Part VII) operates the method. The method is supported by a number of guidelines and techniques (documented in TOGAF, Part III). This produces content to be stored in the repository (documented in TOGAF, Part IV), which is classified according to the Enterprise Continuum (documented in TOGAF, Part V). The repository is initially populated with the TOGAF Reference Models (documented in TOGAF, Part VI).

4 Target audience

Enterprise architects, business architects, IT architects, data architects, systems architects, solutions architects; architecture service providers and tools suppliers.

5 Scope

TOGAF can be used for developing a broad range of different Enterprise Architectures.

TOGAF complements, and can be used in conjunction with, other frameworks that are more focused on specific deliverables for particular vertical sectors such as Government, Telecommunications, Manufacturing, Defense, and Finance. The key to TOGAF is the method – the TOGAF Architecture Development Method (ADM) – for developing an Enterprise Architecture that addresses business needs.

TOGAF covers the development of four related types of architecture. These four types of architecture are commonly accepted as subsets of an overall Enterprise Architecture, all of which TOGAF is designed to support. They are shown on the following page.

Architecture Type	Description
Business Architecture	The business strategy, governance, organization, and key business processes.
Data Architecture	The structure of an organization's logical and physical data assets and data management resources.
Application Architecture	A blueprint for the individual applications to be deployed, their interactions, and their relationships to the core business processes of the organization.
Technology Architecture	The logical software and hardware capabilities that are required to support the deployment of business, data, and application services. This includes IT infrastructure, middleware, networks, communications, processing, and standards.

6 Relevant website

www.opengroup.org/togaf

business management

Balanced Scorecard

1 Title/current version

Balanced Scorecard

2 The basics

The Balanced Scorecard is a strategic planning and management framework that is used to "align business activities to the vision and strategy of the organization, improve internal and external communications, and monitor organization performance against strategic goals" (source: Balanced Scorecard Institute).

3 Summary

The Balanced Scorecard was first published in 1992 by Robert Kaplan (Harvard Business School) and David Norton as a performance measurement framework that added strategic non-financial performance measures to traditional financial metrics to give managers and executives a more 'balanced' view of organizational performance. The Balanced Scorecard has evolved from its early use as a simple performance measurement 'dashboard' to a full strategic planning and management system. It transforms an organization's strategic plan from a passive document into the 'marching orders' for the organization on a daily basis.

The Balanced Scorecard is a management system (not only a measurement system) that enables organizations to clarify their vision and strategy and translate these into action. It provides feedback around both the internal business processes and external outcomes in order to continuously improve strategic performance and results.

The Balanced Scorecard has four perspectives (see Figure):

1. The Learning and Growth Perspective: employee training and corporate cultural attitudes related to both individual and corporate self-improvement.
2. The Business Process Perspective: internal business processes.
3. The Customer Perspective: customer focus and customer satisfaction.
4. The Financial Perspective: financial and financial-related data, such as risk assessment and cost-benefit data.

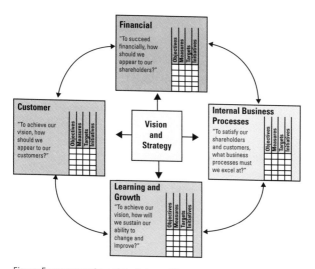

Figure: Four perspectives of the Balanced Scorecard
(Adapted from Robert S. Kaplan and David P. Norton, "Using the Balanced Scorecard as a Strategic Management System," Harvard Business Review (January-February 1996): 76.;)

A Balanced Scorecard should be enhanced with cause-and-effect relationships between measures: outcome measures (lag indicators of past performance) and performance drivers (lead indicators). A well-developed scorecard should contain a good mix of these two metrics.

4 Target audience

Senior management, strategic planners, business managers.

5 Scope and constraints

The Balanced Scorecard was initially developed at an enterprise level. It can easily be adapted to align IT projects, IT departments and IT performance to the needs of the business.

- The Balanced Scorecard is used extensively in business and industry, government and non-profit organizations worldwide
- Use of an IT Balanced Scorecard is one of the most effective means to support the board and management in achieving IT and business alignment

Constraints:

- Visions and strategies that are not actionable
- Strategies that are not linked to departmental, team and individual goals
- Strategies that are not linked to long- and short-term resource allocation
- Feedback that is tactical, not strategic

6 Relevant website

www.balancedscorecard.org

BiSL®

1 Title/current version

BiSL® (Business Information Services Library) 2nd Edition

2 The basics

BiSL (Business Information Services Library) is a framework and collection of best practices for business information management.

3 Summary

BiSL (Business Information Services Library) was developed by a Dutch IT service provider, PinkRoccade and made public in 2005. BiSL was then transferred to the public domain and adopted by the ASL BiSL Foundation. The current version is the 2nd Edition, published in 2012.

BiSL focuses on how business organizations can improve control over their information systems: demand for business support, use of information systems and contracts and other arrangements with IT suppliers. BiSL offers guidance in business information management: support for the use of information systems in the business processes, operational IT control and information management.

The library consists of a framework, best practices, standard templates and a self-assessment. The BiSL framework gives a description of all the processes that enable the control of information systems from a business perspective (see Figure).

The framework distinguishes seven process clusters, which are positioned at the operational, managing and strategic levels (see Figure).

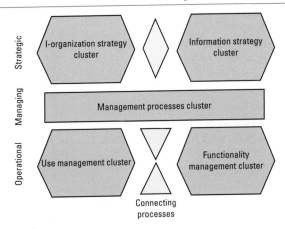

Figure: The process model of BiSL

The *use management* cluster provides optimum, on-going support for the relevant business processes. The *functionality management* cluster structures and effects changes in information provision. The *connecting processes* cluster focuses on decision-making related to which changes need to be made to the information provision, and how they are implemented within the user organization.

The *management processes* cluster ensures that all the activities within the business information management domain are managed in an integrated way.

There are three clusters at the strategic level, which are concerned with the formulation of policies for information provision and the organizations involved in this activity.

4 Target audience

BiSL is primarily aimed at business management, information management and professionals who wish to improve the support of their business processes by realizing a better automated and non-automated information provision.

5 Scope and constraints

The scope of BiSL is the support, usage, maintenance, renovation and policy of the information provision and the management of all related activities

Strengths

- It offers a stable framework and a common language for business information management
- It is supported by a not-for-profit, vendor-independent foundation in which a wide range of organizations participate
- It fills the gap between the business and IT functions. BiSL recognizes and addresses management issues that are increasingly important.

Constraints

- BiSL is relatively new, and therefore relatively unknown outside the Netherlands

6 Relevant website

www.aslbislfoundation.org

BiSL® Next

1 Title

BiSL® Next - A framework for Business Information Management.

2 The Basics

BiSL Next provides an introduction about Business Information Management (BIM) in a pragmatic way and is written for anyone that wants to start practicing BIM, or needs a basic knowledge about key BIM topics. Besides the specific topic of having to deal with digitization of just about everything, attention is given to the organization and governance of BIM. This includes people, technology, and processes essential for business information services.

3 Summary

BiSL Next describes the framework of the next generation of the Business Information Services Library, BiSL®. BiSL Next is a public domain standard for business information management with guiding principles, good practices and practical templates. It offers guidance for *digitally engaged business leaders* and those who collaborate with them. With the ultimate goal to improve business performance through better use of information and technology.

The guidance offers a complete overview of BIM with equal attention for Governance, Strategy, Improvement and Operation of business information services. BiSL® Next has been designed around the concept of continuous improvement and structured in a way that promotes rapid understanding at all levels of business and IT from the Boardroom to the data centre.

Guidance is structured around the four major domains:
Governance, Strategy, Improvement and Operation and covers;

- Definitions and concepts
- Context of the organization
- Policies and the organization of Business Information Management
- Perspectives (from the standpoint of Business, Data, Service and Technology)
- Data Assets
- Responsibilities
- BIM drivers (Need and Value, Capability and Mission)
- Context of other complementary best practices (e.g. ITIL®, COBIT®, TOGAF®)
- Communications
- Implementation ideas.

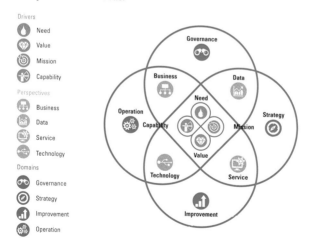

Twelve elements – four drivers, four domains and four perspectives – are the basis of the guidance in BiSL Next. The book also provides checklists and recommendations. Best practice should not be viewed as 'one size fits all'. So it advised that all the guidance should be adapted for the organization in which you work. In addition there are numerous surreal cartoons and quotations that make many of the more esoteric concepts easy to grasp.

4 Target Audience

- **Managers** – who are primarily responsible for implementing and governing digitised services and/or BIM in their organizations and institutions.
- **Data and Information Professionals** – that need to understand the concepts
- **Executives** – who are primarily responsible for developing and/ or approving digitisation and /or BIM governance and strategy and then overseeing its implementation and governance (The "C" suite of Corporate Officers)
- **Academics, Graduates and upper level undergraduate students** – who must teach and master a fundamental understanding of the concepts
- **Everyone within an organization** – who wants to know more about information and data management.

5 Scope
A detailed and pragmatic guide to the concepts of BIM and to the impact of IT on business information services.

6 Relevant reading
https://www.vanharen.net/shop/978940180039c-bislr-next-a-framework-for-business-information-management/

eSCM-CL

1 Title/current version

eSCM-CL (eSourcing Capability Model for Client Organizations)
Version 1.11

2 The basics

eSCM-CL is a 'best practices' capability model for **client**
organizations seeking to improve their capabilities and
relationships when sourcing IT-enabled services; it complements
the eSCM-SP for **service providers**.

3 Summary

eSCM-CL is owned and supported by ITSqc, a spin-off from
Carnegie Mellon University. Version 1.0 was released in 2006;
the current version is Version 1.11 (2010). The model has two
purposes: to give client organizations guidance that will help
them improve their capability across the sourcing lifecycle, and to
provide these organizations with an objective means of evaluating
their sourcing capability.

It is organized into Capability Areas covering major areas of
sourcing expertise, with 95 Practices that address the critical
capabilities needed by clients of IT-enabled services. Each
Practice is arranged along three dimensions: Sourcing Lifecycle,
Capability Area, and Capability Level. The Sourcing Lifecycle is
divided into Analysis, Initiation, Delivery, and Completion, plus
Ongoing, which spans the entire Sourcing Lifecycle.

The seventeen Capability Areas are logical groupings of
Practices that help users to remember and intellectually manage
the content of the Model. The five Capability Levels, numbered

1 through 5, describe an improvement path that progresses from a limited capability to perform sourcing up to the highest level of sustaining excellence over time in the client organization's sourcing activities.

4 Target audience
Client organizations who procure or source IT-enabled services.

5 Scope and constraints
eSCM-CL relates to IT-enabled services. It addresses a full range of client-organization tasks, ranging from developing the organization's sourcing strategy, planning for sourcing and service provider selection, initiating an agreement with service providers, managing service delivery, and completing the agreement. Organizations can be certified to the eSCM-CL.

Strengths
eSCM is twofold: eSCM-CL for Clients and eSCM-SP for Service Providers. These two models are consistent, symmetrical and complementary for each side of the client-provider relationship and this is the strength and the uniqueness of this model. Both models have been used to ensure alignment of processes to build stronger partnership relationships, focus on the primary objectives of the sourcing initiative and sourcing strategy, whether outsourcing, insourcing or shared services.

Constraints
- Fails to define the client organization structure; rather provides guidance to develop the sourcing functions and its workforce
- Emphasis on innovation is present; but assumes that stabilized relationships and governance of service provision come first (e.g. tactical first, strategic later)

- Provides requirements (e.g. practices) for establishing
  sourcing processes, rather than providing sourcing processes
  as is the case with other frameworks, such as ITIL

6 Relevant website

www.itsqc.org

eSCM-CL Model:
www.vanharen-library.net/9789087535599

eSCM-SP

1 Title/current version

eSCM-SP (eSourcing Capability Model for Service Providers)
Version 2

2 The basics

eSCM-SP is a 'best practice' capability model for **service providers** in IT-enabled sourcing, which can be used as both an improvement roadmap and as a certification standard; it complements eSCM-CL for **clients**.

3 Summary

eSCM-SP is owned and supported by ITSqc, a spin-off from Carnegie Mellon University. Version 1.0 was released in 2001; the current version is Version 2.02 (2009). The model has three purposes: to give service providers guidance that will help them improve their capability across the sourcing lifecycle, to provide clients with an objective means of evaluating the capability of service providers, and to offer service providers a standard to use when differentiating themselves from competitors.

Each of the Model's 84 Practices is distributed along three dimensions: Sourcing Lifecycle, Capability Area, and Capability Level. Capability Areas provide logical groupings of Practices to help users better remember and intellectually manage the content of the Model. Service providers can then build or demonstrate capabilities in a particular critical-sourcing function. The ten Capability Areas are Knowledge Management, People Management, Performance Management, Relationship Management, Technology Management, Threat Management,

Service Transfer, Contracting, Service Design & Deployment, and Service Delivery.

The five eSCM-SP Capability Levels indicate the level of an organization's capability. Level 1 indicates that the organization is providing a service. A Level 2 organization has procedures in place to enable it to consistently meet its clients' requirements. At Level 3, an organization is able to manage its performance consistently across engagements. Level 4 requires that an organization is able to add value to its services through innovation. Service providers at Level 5 have proven that they can sustain excellence over a period of at least two years, and have demonstrated this through successive certifications.

4 Target audience
Providers of IT-enabled services and their clients; regardless of whether the service provider is an in-house provider, a shared services unit, or an outsourced or offshore service provider.

5 Scope and constraints
The guidance provided in the eSCM-SP can be applied by providers of IT-enabled services in almost all market sectors and service areas. The eSCM-SP has been designed to complement existing quality models.

Strengths
Most quality models focus only on design and delivery capabilities: the eSCM-SP's Sourcing Lifecycle includes Delivery, and also Initiation and Completion of the contract. The two phases are often the ones most critical to successful sourcing relationships. The Sourcing Lifecycle also includes Overall Practices, which span these Lifecycle phases. eSCM is twofold:

eSCM-CL for Clients and eSCM-SP for Service Providers. These two models are consistent, symmetrical and complementary for each side of the client-provider relationship and this is the strength and the uniqueness of this model. Both models have been used to ensure alignment of processes to build stronger partnerships.

Constraints
- Failing to define exact measures to be collected; the eSCM-SP requires that organizations define the measures that they wish to collect in order to manage their service delivery and relationships
- Provides requirements (e.g. practices) for establishing service management processes, rather than providing processes as is the case with other frameworks, such as ITIL

6 Relevant website

www.itsqc.org

OPBOK

1 Title/current version

OPBOK (Outsourcing Professional Body of Knowledge) Version 10

2 The basics

OPBOK (Outsourcing Professional Body of Knowledge) provides a set of best practices from around the globe for the design, implementation and management of outsourcing contracts, including a code of ethics and business practices for outsourcing professionals.

3 Summary

OPBOK (Outsourcing Professional Body of Knowledge) is owned and maintained by the International Association of Outsourcing Professionals (IAOP). which was formed in 2005 by a consortium of leading companies involved in outsourcing as customers, providers, and advisors. OPBOK was first published in 2006; the current version is Version 10, which reflects major updates from IAOP of the commonly accepted practices and skills required to ensure outsourcing success. It is the basis for IAOP's Certified Outsourcing Professional® qualification and certification programmes.

OPBOK describes the generally accepted set of knowledge and practices applicable to the successful design, implementation, and management of outsourcing contracts. It provides:

- A framework for understanding what outsourcing is and how it fits within business operations
- The knowledge and practice areas generally accepted as critical to outsourcing success

- A glossary of terms commonly used in outsourcing deals and contracts

OPBOK is divided into ten knowledge areas covering major areas of outsourcing expertise. The OPBOK framework is based on a five-stage outsourcing process (see Figure).

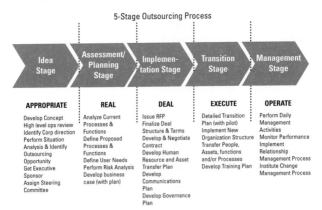

5-Stage Outsourcing Process

APPROPRIATE	**REAL**	**DEAL**	**EXECUTE**	**OPERATE**
Develop Concept	Analyze Current	Issue RFP	Detailed Transition	Perform Daily
High level ops review	Processes &	Finalize Deal	Plan (with pilot)	Management
Identify Corp direction	Functions	Structure & Terms	Implement New	Activities
Perform Situation	Define Proposed	Develop & Negotiate	Organization Structure	Monitor Performance
Analysis & Identify	Processes &	Contract	Transfer People,	Implement
Outsourcing	Functions	Develop Human	Assets, functions	Relationship
Opportunity	Define User Needs	Resource and Asset	and/or Processes	Management Process
Get Executive	Perform Risk Analysis	Transfer Plan	Develop Training Plan	Institute Change
Sponsor	Develop business	Develop		Management Process
Assign Steering	case (with plan)	Communications		
Committee		Plan		
		Develop Governance		
		Plan		

Figure: OPBOK five-stage outsourcing process
Source: IAOP

4 Target audience

Targeted principally at outsourcing professionals who are buyers, providers and advisors in the outsourcing industry; also of interest to senior management in buying organizations; trainers and academics addressing outsourcing topics.

5 Scope and constraints

The scope of OPBOK is governance and defining a strategic approach to outsourcing, governance, identifying and communicating business requirements, selecting and qualifying

providers, gaining internal buy-in, creating project teams, and getting value for money and return on investment.

OPBOK and Carnegie Mellon's eSourcing Capability Models (eSCMs) are becoming the most relevant outsourcing standards. OPBOK complements eSCM-CL (eSCM for clients). OPBOK focuses on outsourcing of any service (but only outsourcing). eSCM-CL focuses on sourcing of IT-enabled services and covers multiple types of sourcing, including outsourcing, insourcing, and shared services. OPBOK is used as the basis for individual certification – the Certified Outsourcing Professional (COP), while eSCM-CL supports organizational appraisal, evaluation, and certification.

Strengths

OPBOK reflects the best practice of outsourcing professionals worldwide, including the 'make or break' factors that can affect any outsourcing initiative.

Constraints

OPBOK does not address insourcing or shared services.

6 Relevant website

www.iaop.org

Operating Model Canvas

1 Title

Operating Model Canvas: Aligning operations and organization with strategy

2 The basics

Operating Model Canvas describes a tool that managers can use to help them achieve alignment with strategy and with each other. It presents many examples from Uber to Shell to an IT function to a charity. It includes a toolbox of nearly 20 tools that help analyse and define an operating model. It also has two fully worked case studies.

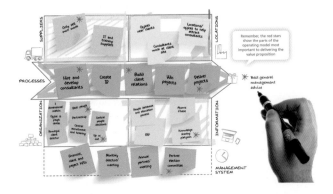

The Operating Model Canvas dovetails with the Business Model Canvas. As Yves Pigneur, author of Business Model Generation and Value Proposition Design explains "Andrew Campbell and co-authors have focused on the left-hand side of the Business Model Canvas for creating an Operating Model Canvas." Patrick van der Pijl, author of Design a Better Business added "This

book is part of a family of books – Business Model Generation, Value Proposition Design and Design a better Business. They should all be in your bookshelf or on the side of your desk."

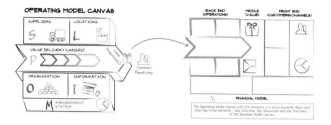

3 Summary

An operating model is a document. It helps high level management to convert strategy into operational implications. Think of a building blueprint.

An operating model helps senior managers make operational choices. It helps the head of operations design the detailed work processes. It helps the head of HR decide what sort of people are needed to do the work and what sort of structure is needed to guide and control them. It helps the head of IT make decisions about IT architecture. It helps the head of supply chain design relationships with suppliers. So an operating model is an important step between strategy and all the decisions that need to be made to create a functioning organization.

A high-level operating model can be a single page. Of course there are operating models of 100 pages and operating manuals of more than 1000 pages. Though this book is about high-level models.

The Operating Model Canvas is a one-page model. For those familiar with the Business Model Canvas, the Operating Model Canvas covers the operating elements (Activities, Resources and Partners) with six elements that make up the mnemonic POLISM – Processes, Organisation, Locations, Information, Suppliers and Management system.

Processes for the work that needs to be done to deliver a value proposition or service proposition to a customer/beneficiary: the value delivery chain. Organization for people who will do the work, the structure, the functions needed to support the work and the decision powers given to people in the structure. Location for where the work is done. Information for the software applications needed to support the work. Suppliers for those outside the organization whose engagement is also needed. Management system for planning, budgeting, performance monitoring and controls needed to run the organization.

It is possible to create an Operating Model Canvas for a multinational company, for a single business, for a function like HR or sales within a business, for a department within a function, for a charity and for a government body.

The book shows you how to create an Operating Model Canvas and provides dozens of examples of all different types of Canvases.

Chapter 1 – Operating Model Canvas
Describes the link with the Business Model Canvas and the role that an Operating Model Canvas plays in a transformation journey

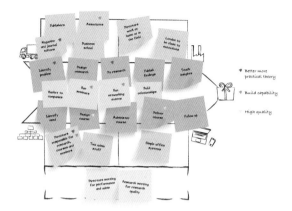

Chapter 2 – Operating Model Canvas examples
15 examples of real organizations from Uber to Shell to an IT function to Cardboard Citizens
Chapter 3 – Toolbox
18 tools divided between 5 core tools and 13 additional tools
Chapter 4 – Designing a target operating model for a business
Fully worked example of a company in the business of supplying equipment to the electricity transmission industry
Chapter 5 – Designing an operating model for a function
Fully worked example of an IT function
Chapter 6 – Change examples
Six 'as is' and 'to be' examples that improved performance

4 Target Audience
- A manager in operations or in any function who wants to design how the operation works
- A CEO or COO or entrepreneur who wants to review his or her organization and plans

- A lean practitioner or process excellence manager who wants to be more strategic
- A manager in strategy or planning who wants to make the plans more practical
- A project manager or change specialist working on a transformation project
- A leader who wants to make sure her team members are all on the same page
- A business partner in HR, IT or Finance who wants to improve the business
- A business development manager who wants to design a new business
- A Business Architect, Enterprise Architect or Operations Strategist
- A manager tasked with cutting costs or improving service or quality
- A customer experience or user experience specialist
- A manager in charge of post merger integration
- A consultant helping organizations improve
- Anyone responsible for performance

5 Scope

- What is an operating model?
- The link between operating models and business models
- The link between operating models and strategy
- The tools of operating model design
- How to design a target operating model
- Fully worked examples of operating model design
- The role of an operating model in transformation

6 Relevant website

https://www.vanharen.net/shop/978940180071c-operating-model
-canvas/

Six Sigma

1 Title/current version

Six Sigma

2 The basics

Six Sigma is a structured, disciplined and rigorous approach and method for process improvement through identifying and eliminating defects. Six Sigma is a business management strategy, originally developed by Motorola, USA in 1986.

3 Summary

The use of Six Sigma as a measurement standard is based on the concept of the normal curve, dating from the 1920s, when Walter Shewhart demonstrated that three sigma (standard deviations) from the mean is a point where a process requires correction. In the mid-1980s Motorola engineers started to measure defects in millions per opportunities to provide adequate detail in measuring quality levels. The term 'Six Sigma' was coined in that period by one of the engineers involved, Bill Smith of Motorola.

Six Sigma refers to the statistical notion of having a 99.99 per cent confidence of achieving specified results. A greater sigma implies a lower expected Defects per Million Opportunities (DMO) for defect or error. The statistical representation of Six Sigma describes quantitatively how a process is performing. To achieve Six Sigma a process must not produce more than 3.4 defects per million opportunities, where a defect is defined as anything outside customer specifications.

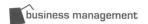

Six Sigma can be perceived at three levels:

1. Metric: Defects Per Million Opportunities (DPMO).
2. Methodology:
   – DMAIC (Define-Measure-Analyze-Improve-Control) is a structured problem solving roadmap and tools
   – DMADV (Define-Measure-Analyze-Design-Verify) is a data-driven quality strategy for designing product and processes
   – DFSS (Design For Six Sigma) is an approach for the deployment of Six Sigma.
3. Philosophy: reduce variation in the business and take customer-focused, data-driven decisions by implementing a measurement-based strategy that focuses on process improvement and variation reduction through the application of Six Sigma improvements projects.

Six Sigma uses a set of quality management techniques, including statistical information, and creates a unique infrastructure of people within the organization ('Black Belts', 'Green Belts', etc.) who are experts in Six Sigma. Each Six Sigma project carried out within an organization follows a defined sequence of steps and has quantified project targets (such as cost reduction and/or profit increase).

4 Target audience

Six Sigma can be used by anybody who is involved in process improvement such as business analysts, engineers, project managers and advisors.

5 Scope and constraints

The scope of Six Sigma is any process in any type of organization – from manufacturing to transactions and from product to service

where an approach and methodology is needed for eliminating defects.

Six Sigma is complementary to 'Lean' approaches, which focus on the elimination of wasteful process activities. Some practitioners have combined Six Sigma ideas with Lean thinking to create a method called Lean Six Sigma.

Strengths
- A secure, rigorous and structured method
- A fact-based approach (statistical instead of based on intuition)
- Trained resources with appropriate skills
- Fast implementation

Constraints
- Using Six Sigma for processes with a low volume of output. This can produce unreliable results
- Not enough statistical knowledge available in order to be able to use sophisticated statistical methods. Extensive training is needed for correct use of the approach

6 Relevant website

www.isssp.com

SqEME®

1 Title/current version

SqEME® Process Management, SqEME Edition 2008

2 The basics

SqEME® is an open standard for developing process-centered architectures of an enterprise; it views processes from the perspectives of four complementary 'windows'. It is owned by the not-for-profit organization *Stichting SqEME* in the Netherlands.

3 Summary

SqEME® was developed by a Dutch network of private and public organizations, consultancy agencies and independent advisors. SqEME was first published in 2002 and in 2007 the SqEME Foundation was established. The current version of SqEME is Edition 2008.

SqEME enables organizations to recognize, design, control, manage and improve their processes; it also supplies a set of consistent and coherent modeling techniques. A key assumption in the method is the professional maturity of the employee. The focus is not on what the employee has to do in detail, but on the surrounding system. It is on cooperation and the flow of information between employees. It investigates how the different parts of the organization are tuned to each other and how the intra-organization messaging takes place.

The thinking model that forms the basis of the SqEME® method is visualized by means of four 'windows'. These four windows are called Constitution, Chemistry, Construction and Correspondence (see Figure).

The Constitution window is concerned with questions of a 'constitutional nature':

- What are the key result areas of the enterprise?
- What are the activities that can be distinguished within the key result areas?
- What interaction patterns connect the constituent activities?

The Correspondence window is used to obtain a picture of the dynamics of the enterprise 'in operation'. It is about monitoring the business. Do business processes proceed as visualized and agreed upon, and do the processes perform in line with their objectives?

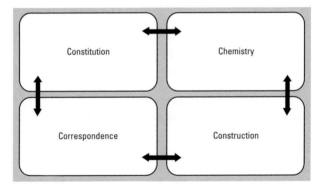

Figure: The SqEME windows
Source: SqEME

The Chemistry window concentrates on the 'cohesion' in the enterprise, the interaction between the involved professionals. This window shows primarily the quality of the interaction and the communication patterns.

The Construction window offers the most tangible view on the enterprise with a focus on deployment and implementation. These four windows make it possible to look at organizations differently –not the vertical lines of the hierarchical structure, but the processes and their interrelatedness within the organization.

4 Target audience
Anyone who is involved in business process modeling and process improvement.

5 Scope and constraints
The scope of SqEME is process improvement enterprise-wide.

Strengths
- The SqEME® method makes it possible to describe the design of an organization in a subtle but unambiguous way. It also offers a complete set of consistent and coherent modeling techniques
- The method has proven itself in practice. SqEME® is being applied in Dutch organizations within the industrial, service and not-for-profit sectors

Constraints
It can take a long time to model all the business processes in a detailed way. One of the main messages is 'Good is good enough'.

6 Relevant website
www.sqeme.org (Dutch only)

Our global knowledge partners include:

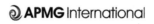

Please Note

All titles are published in English unless otherwise indicated. All
ISBNs indicate the English edition. ISBNs for all of our published and
forthcoming titles, including non-English editions, are available on our
website. All prices are shown in euros excl. VAT and are correct as
of January 2016. They are excluding tax and delivery, and may be
subject to change. Currency conversions into non-euro denominations

adopt the current exchange rate on the day on which the order is processed, so some prices may be subject to the fluctuations in the exchange rate. Please note covers are for illustration purposes. FREE! Sample chapters from all of our titles can be viewed on our website at **www.vanharen.net** or via the Amazon LookInside and Google Book Search initiatives.

READ

IT

ON

ANY

DEVICE

The Van Haren Publishing portfolio

Our portfolio offers information regarding Best Practices and worldwide standards. This information is made available to you through different formats:

The eKnowledge base offers free access into our unique collection of Best Practices whitepapers. Additionally, practice exams can be downloaded and Best Practices templates are available to support the implementation of frameworks within your organization.

eLibrary

The eLibrary contains all information on:

- IT & IT Management (ITIL, ASL and BiSL)
- Project Management (PRINCE2 and PMBoK)
- Enterprise Architecture (TOGAF and ArchiMate)
- Business Management (ISO 20000, 27001/2)

Here you can download the most recent and up-to-date eBook publication to stay completely informed regarding the latest developments within your area of expertise.

The eShop allows you to browse through all titles, offering summaries, indexes and even expert recommendations. When you have made your choice, you can place your order in your favorite media format: Hard copy, eBook or ePub.

All prices mentioned in this catalog are excluding tax and shipping

IT Service Management Based on ITIL® 2011 Edition

ISBN 978 94 018 0017 4

English €34,95

Languages: English, Dutch
Available formats: Hard copy, eBook

- An easy-to-read introduction into the entire ITIL Library
- Covers all specifications of AXELOS' syllabus for the ITIL 2011 Edition Foundation certification
- Covers all processes in ITIL 2011 Edition

Reader's comments:

'Well written and presented, this publication provides a useful addition to the core ITIL publications for anyone wanting to understand IT service management.'
Kevin Holland, Service Management Specialist, NHS
'Pierre has produced an extremely useful summary of the current version of ITIL. This will be an invaluable day to day reference for all practitioners.
'Claire Agutter, ITIL Training Zone

ITIL® 2011 Edition – A Pocket Guide
ISBN 978 90 8753 676 3

- New version of this bestselling title based on ITIL 2011 Edition, formally licensed by AXELOS
- Save time: get the key points of ITIL 2011 in this concise pocket guide
- Quality content, also great as study material for ITIL Foundation exam

Languages: English, German, Dutch
Available formats: Hard copy, eBook, ePub

IT Service-portfoliomanagement: Maximaliseer de waarde van IT
ISBN 978 90 8753 644 2

- Het ontwikkelen en beheren van een portfolio aan (IT-)diensten
- Vele herkenbare voorbeelden, zowel binnen als buiten de IT
- Maximaliseer de waarde van IT voor uw onderneming

Languages: Nederlands
Available formats: Hard copy, eBook

The ITIL Process Manual
ISBN 978 90 8753 650 3

- Written by Global expert
- Implementation of Major ITIL processes
- Best practice interfaces between processes
- Practical guidance with great templates
- Peer reviewed by major experts worldwide for great quality
- Popular title used around the globe

Languages: English
Available formats: Hard copy, eBook

The IT Service Part 1 – The Essentials
ISBN 978 90 8753 667 1

- A complete repository of all you need to know about IT Service Management
- References the world's leading approaches
- Peer reviewed for quality
- Global applications

English
€39,95

Languages: English
Available formats: Hard copy, eBook

The IT Service Part 2 – The Handbook
ISBN 978 90 8753 700 5

- A complete repository of all you need to know about IT Service Management
- References the world's leading approaches
- Peer reviewed for quality
- Global applications

English
€39,95

Languages: English
Available formats: Hard copy, eBook

ISO/IEC 20000:2011 – A Pocket Guide
ISBN 978 90 8753 726 5

- A Pocket Guide to ISO 20000, the new IT service management standard
- A well-known standard adopted by many organizations globally
- Key content great for EXIN and TÜV SÜD exam preparation
- Popular title used around the globe

English
€15,95

Languages: English
Available formats: Hard copy, eBook

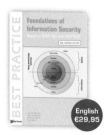

Languages: English,
Dutch
Available formats:
Hard copy, eBook

Foundations of Information Security
Based on ISO27001 and ISO27002 –
3rd revised edition
ISBN 978 94 018 0012 9

- This book is intended for everyone in an
  organization who wishes to have a basic
  understanding of information security. The
  information security concepts in this revised
  edition are based on the ISO/IEC27001:2013
  and ISO/IEC27002:2013 standards. But
  the text also refers to the other relevant
  international standards for information security
- This book is primarily developed as a study
  book for anyone who wants to pass the ISFS
  (Information Security Foundation) exam of EXIN.
  In an appendix an ISFS model exam is given,
  with feedback to all multiple choice options
- Also available in Dutch:
  ISBN 978 94 018 0013 6

Languages: Nederlands
Available formats:
Hard copy, eBook

Basiskennis informatiebeveiliging op
basis van ISO27001 en ISO27002 -
2e herziene druk
ISBN 978 94 018 0013 6

- De tweede druk is een ingrijpende herziening
  van de eerste druk (uit 2010), waarbij de
  inhoud is aangepast aan de nieuwe versie van
  de standaards: ISO/IEC 27001:2013 en ISO/
  IEC 27002:2013
- Het bevat de basiskennis die onmisbaar is voor
  iedereen die beroepsmatig betrokken is bij
  informatiebeveiliging of IT

Languages: English
Available formats:
Hard copy, eBook

ABC of ICT – An Introduction

The Official ABC Introduction

ISBN 978 90 8753 142 3

- Covers 'Attitude, Behavior and Culture' concepts that are critical to make ICT really happen
- 35 fantastic case studies and examples from industry experts of where things can go wrong – and how to make them right
- Used globally by leading consultants and trainers in the field
- The sister publication to the well-known ABC Card Deck and the new ABC of ICT Exercise steps in solving them

Languages: English
Available formats: Hard copy, eBook, ePub

ABC of ICT – The Exercise Workbook

ISBN 978 90 8753 142 3

- A great training tool to use to identify your team improvement needs
- The exercises can be integrated into your ITIL and ITSM Training
- Helps develop the people skills vital to realizing successful ICT Change

Languages: English, Chinese, Russian
Available formats: Hard copy, eBook

Metrics for IT Service Management

ISBN 978 90 77212 69 1

- Approach to measuring deliverables within Service Management operations
- A general guide to the design, implementation and use of metrics
- Contains practical sheets for immediate day-to-day use

Metrics for IT Service Management: Designing for ITIL®

ISBN 978 90 8753 648 0

- Practical Metrics for ITIL and ISO 20000 Implementation
- Best Practice Guidance for use within Service Operations
- Written by the Author of the Industry 'Bible': Metrics for IT Service Management

English
€39,95

Languages: English
Available formats: Hard copy, eBook

COBIT ® 5 – A Management Guide

ISBN 978 90 8753 701 2

- This book provides an overview of IT Governance and is a quick reference guide to COBIT® 5 for people that are not acquainted with this field of work
- It provides trainers and students a compact reference to COBIT® 5
- Quality reviewed by experts from around the world

English
€22,50

Languages: English
Available formats: Hard copy, eBook

Scrum – A Pocket Guide
ISBN 978 90 8753 720 3

- A practical introduction into Scrum
- A complete overview of all Scrum fundamentals
- Essential study aid for training for Scrum certifications:
  - Certified Scrum Master (ScrumAlliance)
  - Certified Scrum Product Owner (ScrumAlliance)
  - Professional Scrum Foundations (PSF, Scrum.org)

Languages: English, Dutch
Available formats: Hard copy, eBook, ePub

Agile – Pocketguide voor Agile organisaties
ISBN 978 90 8753 798 2

- Snelle, overzichtelijke introductie tot Agile
- Eén van de weinige Nederlandstalige Agile boeken met Nederlandse voorbeelden
- Informatie voor verschillende rollen: IT, algemeen management, projectmanagement

Lanaguages: Nederlands
Available formats: Hard copy, eBook

Informatieanalyse voor Engineering en Management van Requirements
ISBN 978 94 018 0029 7

- Dit boek richt zich op de business-/informatie-analist. Het reikt hem of haar alles aan wat nodig is om business requirements boven water te halen, te analyseren, te beschrijven, oplossingsrichtingen ervoor te zoeken en alternatieven uit te werken inclusief business cases
- In dit traject zijn modellen van bedrijfsprocessen en datamodellen essentieel in de communicatie tussen ontwerpers en belanghebbenden. De modelleertaal is UML (Unified Modeling Language), het ontwikkelproces is gebaseerd op RUP (Rational Unified Process)

Languages: Nederlands
Available formats:
Hard copy, eBook

Languages: English
Available formats:
Hard copy, eBook

SIAM: Principles and Practices for Service Integration and Management
ISBN 978 94 018 0025 9

- This is the first book that describes the concepts of Service Integration and Management (SIAM) as a new approach
- Service Integration is the set of principles and practices, which facilitate the collaborative working relationships between service providers required to maximize the benefit of multi-sourcing
- Service integration facilitates the linkage of services, the technology of which they are comprised and the delivery organizations and processes used to operate them, into a single operating model

Languages: English
Available formats:
Hard copy, eBook

Service Integration and Management Foundation Body of Knowledge (SIAM® Foundation BoK)
ISBN 978 94 018 0102 7

- This book introduces service integration and management (SIAM). Its contents are the source material for the EXIN BCS Service Integration and Management Foundation (SIAM®F) certification
- Service integration and management (SIAM) is a management methodology that can be applied in an environment that includes services sourced from a number of service providers
- SIAM introduces the concept of a service integrator, which is a single, logical entity held accountable for the end to end delivery of services and the business value that the customer receives
- The second part of the book contains the SIAM Process Guides. This is a (not exhaustive) list of processes that support SIAM. Its aim is to identify SIAM considerations for common processes used in a SIAM environment, not to describe each process in detail

Languages: English
Available formats:
Hard copy, eBook

IT Capability Maturity Framework™ (IT-CMF™)

ISBN 978 94 018 0027 3

- The IT Capability Maturity Framework™ (IT-CMF™) is a comprehensive suite of tried and tested practices, organizational assessment approaches, and improvement roadmaps covering the full range of capabilities needed to optimize value and innovation in the IT function and the wider organization

- It is an integrated management toolkit covering more than 30 management disciplines, with organizational maturity profiles, assessment methods, and improvement roadmaps for each

Languages: English
Available formats:
Hard copy, eBook

IT-CMF – A Management Guide - Based on the IT Capability Maturity Framework™ (IT-CMF™) 2nd edition

ISBN 978 94 018 0196 6

- This management guide offers an introduction to the IT Capability Maturity Framework™ (IT-CMF™), second edition

- It is an integrated management toolkit covering 36 key capability management disciplines, with organizational maturity profiles, assessment methods, and improvement roadmaps for each

- A coherent set of concepts and principles, expressed in business language, that can be used to guide discussions on setting goals and evaluating performance

- A unifying (or umbrella) framework that complements other, domain-specific frameworks already in use in the organization, helping to resolve conflicts between them, and filling gaps in their coverage

The Service Catalog –
A Practitioner Guide
ISBN 978 90 8753 571 1

- Practical guidance on building a Service Catalog
- Focuses on IT community relationship with the business and users
- Includes practical templates and guidance on key documents such as OLAs and SLAs

Languages: English, Japanese
Available formats: Hard copy, eBook

Six Sigma for IT Management
ISBN 978 90 77212 30 1

- Combining the Six Sigma approach with ITIL best practice
- Coherent view and guidance for using the Six Sigma approach
- A quantitative methodology of continuous improvement

Languages: English, Korean, Chinese
Available formats: Hard copy, eBook

Six Sigma for IT Management
– A Pocket Guide
ISBN 978 90 8753 029 7

- The pocket guide provides succinct guidance and concise explanations
- Merges ITIL and Six Sigma methodologies into a single unified approach
- Based on the introductory guide 'Six Sigma for IT Management'

Languages: English
Available formats: Hard copy, eBook

The IT Factory
ISBN 978 90 8753 686 2

- A complete guide for new approaches to dynamic IT delivery
- Aligns with Supply Chain best practice with practical implementation guidance
- Innovative approach designed to support cloud and virtualization

English
€39,95

Languages: English
Available formats: Hard copy, eBook

IT Outsourcing Part 1:
Contracting the Partner
ISBN 978 90 8753 030 3

- As companies focus on the core specialisms, most will look to the benefits of outsourcing some, if not all, of the IT services required. The benefits include:cost-efficient operations;delivery of IT services at lower cost through economies of scale; improvements in time-to-market of IT solutions; improvements in capability andquality of IT service delivery.

English
€22,50

Languages: English
Available formats: Hard copy, eBook

IT Outsourcing Part 2:
Managing the Sourcing Contract
ISBN 978 90 8753 616 9

- IT Outsourcing Part 2: Managing the Sourcing Contract covers all the processes for managing the contract, from the transition phase through to normal operational service and contract termination
- Developed for IT practitioners as well as commercial and contract managers

English
€22,50

Languages: English
Available formats: Hard copy, eBook

ASL®2 – A Framework for Application Management

ISBN 978 90 8753 313 7

- This book supports the Exam ASL Foundation
- ASL is a publica domain process framework for application management
- This book is the official manual of ASL2, an improved version of the 2001 framework

English
€39,95

Languages: English, Dutch
Available formats: Hard copy, eBook, ePub (Dutch)

ASL®2 – A Pocket Guide

ISBN 978 90 8753 643 5

- ASL2 is an evolutionary improvement on the succesful ASL framework
- Comprehensive introduction to the basic principles of ASL2
- Complementary to other frameworks like BiSL and ITIL

English
€15,95

Languages: English, Dutch
Available formats: Hard copy, eBook

ASL®2 Self-assessment

ISBN 978 90 8753 740 1

- Self-assessment is the individual, systematic review of a way of working and the results of it
- Based on the results of this evaluation actions van be initiated for further improvement

English
€12,95

Languages: English, Dutch
Available formats: Hard copy, eBook

Implementing Information Security Based on ISO 27001/ISO 27002 – A Management Guide

ISBN 978 90 8753 541 4

- Covers the Information Security ISO standards based on ISO 27001 / ISO 27002
- Implementing and achieving certification of internationally recognised ISO standards
- A succinct guide for those requiring a guide to implementation issues

Languages: English
Available formats: Hard copy, eBook

Open Information Security Management Maturity Model (O-ISM3)

ISBN 978 90 8753 665 7

- Supports the common frameworks such as ISO 9000, ISO 27000, COBIT, ITIL and many more
- Published by the well-respected, independent, global organization The Open Group
- Practical process-based approach encourages continuous improvement

Languages: English
Available formats: Hard copy, eBook

Open Enterprise Security Architecture (O-ESA)

A Framework and Template for Policy-Driven Security

ISBN 978 90 8753 672 5

- Covers key policy-driven security approach essential to any organization
- A framework and template on Open Enterprise Security Architecture (O-ESA)
- Published by the well-respected, independent, global organization The Open Group

Languages: English
Available formats: Hard copy, eBook

De ISM-methode
ISBN 978 90 125 8500 2

- De aanleiding voor de ontwikkeling van de ISM-methode: niet het wiel opnieuw uitvinden, maar alle voor IT-dienstverlening relevante en toepasbare kennis en ervaring onderbrengen in één praktische methode. De ISM-methode wordt inmiddels bij een groot en groeiend aantal IT-beheerafdelingen succesvol toegepast

Languages: Nederlands
Available formats: Hard copy, eBook

The ISM method Version 3
ISBN 978 01 17 08106 2

- This book describes a revolutionary approach on how to successfully implement IT service management (ITSM) in an easier, faster, cheaper, and especially more effective way
- This publication describes the implementation method, with a strong focus on quality assurance and cultural change, a comprehensive definition list, and an example of a compact process model

Languages: English
Available formats: Hard copy, eBook

De FSM-methode
A Framework and Template for Policy-Driven Security
ISBN 978 94 917 1001 8

- Dit boek wordt een methodische benadering geboden voor het gestandaardiseerd inrichten en aansturen van modern functioneel beheer
- De opzet van de FSM-methode is geheel analoog aan de ISM-methode voor IT-beheer. De methodes worden door tientallen leveranciers van producten en diensten gebruikt bij het ondersteunen van betere dienstverlening in de praktijk van de informatievoorziening

Languages: Nederlands
Available formats:
Hard copy, eBook

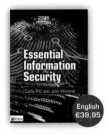

Languages: English
Available formats: Hard copy, eBook

Essential information Security
ISBN 978 90 8753 736 4

* This book covers the most relevant topics like cloud security, mobile device security and network security
* This book provides a comprehensive overview of what is important in information security
* Processes, training strategy, policies, contingency plans, risk management and effectiveness of tools are all extensively discussed

Languages: Nederlands
Available formats:
Hard copy, eBook

Wegwijzer voor evalueren van IT-projecten
ISBN 978 90 8753 725 8

* Dit boek beoogt een heldere classificatie van de meest relevante methoden en best practices te geven, op basis van een interdisciplinaire theoretische basis
* Het boek rijkt daarbij concrete handvatten aan en helpt managers, professionals en bestuurders duidelijke keuzes te maken bij evaluaties van IT-projecten
* Er worden ruim twintig best practices en methoden in dit boek besproken: People: ICB/NCB, e-CF, Belbin teamrollen, Projectmatig creëren; Process: PRINCE2, PMBOK Guide, ISO 21500, Agile methoden (DSDM/Atern, Scrum, RUP), ISO 9000, OPM3; Product: ASL/BiSL/ITIL, Business Case-aanpak, BCG-matrix; Multi-criteria: 7'S model, Quinn-model, INK / EFQM, Appreciative Inquiry, Balanced Scorecard

Languages: English
Available formats:
Hard copy, eBook

Lean IT Partnering
ISBN 978 94 018 0023 5

- This book contains the results of the Nyenrode Lean Institute research project 'Lean IT partnering' and presents experienced barriers and drivers for victory
- Additionally, it provides the lessons learned from actual case studies and postulates suitable guidelines for successful Lean IT partnerships: Craft an adequate partnering strategy, demonstrate Lean Leadership, and apply the appropriate Lean tools and techniques that fit naturally with the objectives sought for the IT partnership at hand

Languages: Nederlands
Available formats:
Hard copy, eBook

Lean IT – Theorie en praktijk van Lean in een IT-omgeving
ISBN 978 94 018 0015 0

- Dit boek is gebaseerd op de bedrijfsbrede toepassing van de negen Lean IT principes, weergegeven in een vijflaagse piramide, zoals beschreven door Bell & Orzen en beschrijft op een heldere en eenduidige wijze:
  - van Lean naar Lean IT
  - de toegevoegde waarde en de toepassing van Lean IT en
  - de integratie in de bestaande organisatiestructuur
- Lean IT heeft alles te maken met klantgerichtheid, integrale ketenbenadering en is sterk gericht op de organisatiecultuur van de IT-omgeving en op de mensen die daarin werken, onder andere door middel van empowerment van medewerkers om hen permanent te betrekken bij het optimaliseren van processen

Languages: English
Available formats:
Hard copy, eBook,
ePub

Implementing Effective IT Governance and IT Management
ISBN 978 94 018 0008 2

- This book offers a comprehensive and integrated approach for IT/Business Alignment, Planning, Execution and Governance. It offers structured and practical solutions using the best of the best practices available today
- The book is divided into two parts, which cover the three critical pillars necessary to develop, execute and sustain a robust and effective IT governance environment:- Leadership, people, organization and strategy,- IT governance, its major component processes and enabling technologies

Languages: Nederlands
Available formats:
Hard copy, eBook

e-CF in de Praktijk
ISBN 978 94 018 0021 1

- In het eerste deel van dit boek worden de opzet en inhoud van het e-CF framework toegelicht, mede in relatie tot andere competentieframeworks, zoals SFIA. Daarbij wordt ook uitleg gegeven over concrete zaken zoals functieprofielen, enz.
- In het tweede deel wordt uitgelegd hoe e-CF in de praktijk kan worden toegepast, gerelateerd aan bestaande kennis en inzichten uit o.a. de testpsychologie, zoals bij het verrichten van assessments
° Er zijn drie casus opgenomen van een praktische toepassing van e-CF, namelijk bij het Rijk (Kwaliteitsraamwerk IV), Nationale politie en Pink Elephant

Project Management Based on PRINCE® 2009 Edition
ISBN 978 90 8753 496 7

- This book is the officially licensed material for PRINCE2 2009 Edition
- Contains lists serving as reference material for all project types and sizes
- Covers all specifications of the Syllabus for the PRINCE2 Foundation exams of AXELOS

Languages: English, Dutch
Available formats: Hard copy, eBook, ePub

PRINCE2® 2009 Edition – A Pocket Guide
ISBN 978 90 8753 544 5

- This pocket guide is based on PRINCE2 2009 Edition
- Quick introduction and structured overview of the PRINCE2 method

Languages: English, Dutch, German, French
Available formats: Hard copy, eBook, ePub (Dutch)

De Projectsaboteur en PRINCE2
ISBN 978 90 8753 666 4

- Dit boek gaat over een jonge projectmanager die de opdracht heeft gekregen om zijn eerste grote project zelfstandig te managen. Hij past daarbij de veel gebruikte projectmanagementmethode PRINCE2 toe
- Een leerzaam boek, zowel voor de projectmanager, als voor de projectsaboteur

Languages: Nederlands
Available formats: Hard copy, eBook

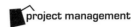 **project management**

Languages: Nederlands
Available formats:
Hard copy, eBook

Projectmanagement voor opdrachtgevers – Management Guide
ISBN 978 90 8753 734 0

- Dit boek helpt je als opdrachtgever een succes van je project te maken met de krachtige en in de praktijk bewezen vier principes van succesvol opdrachtgeverschap
- Dit boek is bestemd voor managers die in de rol van opdrachtgevers verantwoordelijk zijn voor verschillende soorten projecten, zoals onderzoek, productontwikkeling, infrastructurele werken, woningbouw, bedrijfsverhuizingen en IT-projecten

Languages: Nederlands
Available formats: Hard copy, eBook

Basisboek Projectmanagement
ISBN 978 90 8753 716 6

- Bestemd voor iedereen die op een praktische manier kennis wil maken met projectmanagent
- Primair bedoeld voor gebruik in het hoger onderwijs
- Gebaseerd op een doordachte didactische aanpak die aansluit op de beleving van mensen die voor het eerst met een project in aanraking komen

Languages: Nederlands
Available formats: Hard copy, eBook

Organisaties Veranderen met Programma's
Bruggen slaan tussen lijn en projecten
ISBN 978 90 8753 227 7

- Hoe overheid en bedrijfsleven externe uitdagingen en eigen ambities realiseren
- Op basis van onderzoek naar de praktijk van grootschalige verandertrajecten
- Identificatie van de succesfactoren en voorwaarden

Dutch
€29,95

Verandermanagement – Basisprincipes en praktijk
ISBN 978 90 8753 689 3

- Alle belangrijke zaken die te maken hebben met veranderingen in organisaties
- Belangrijkste theorieën en opvattingen over verandermanagement

Languages: Nederlands
Available formats: Hard copy, eBook

English
€15,95

A Pocket Companion to PMI's *PMBOK® Guide* – Fifth edition

PM series

ISBN 978 90 8753 804 0

- Provides a summary of the PMBOK® Guide Fifth Edition
- Deals with key issues and themes within project management and *PMBOK Guide®*
- Updated with the latest PMI organizational information

Languages: English, Dutch, German, Spanish
Available formats: Hard copy, eBook, ePub

Dutch
€39,95

Programmamanagement op basis van MSP® 2011 Edition

ISBN 978 90 8753 691 6

- Deze nieuwe druk is aangepast aan MSP® 2011 Edition
- De inhoud van dit boek is een uitstekende voorbereiding op het MSP® Foundation examen
- Toegankelijke inhoud door de heldere tekst en vele afbeeldingen

Languages: Nederlands
Available formats: Hard copy, eBook

Wegwijzer voor methoden bij Projectmanagement – 2de geheel herziene druk

ISBN 978 90 8753 639 8

- Objectieve vergelijking van de 10 belangrijkste methoden in Nederland
- Combinatie van kwalitatieve en kwantitatieve benadering
- Gefundeerde adviezen om delen van een methode te gebruiken en/of te combineren

Languages: Nederlands
Available formats: Hard copy, eBook

Wegwijzer voor modellen voor organisatievolwassenheid bij projectmanagement

ISBN 978 90 8753 168 3

- Beschrijft individuele kenmerken van de vier belangrijkste volwassenheidsmodellen
- Legt uit hoe de geselecteerde volwassenheidsmodellen zich verhouden
- Geeft aan wat de sterke en zwakke kanten van de geselecteerde volwassenheidsmodellen zijn

Languages: Nederlands
Available formats: Hard copy, eBook

De complete projectmanager

ISBN 978 94 018 0041 9

- Dit boek gaat over het hoe van projectmanagement en hoe je als projectmanager met een proactieve houding ook in moeilijke situaties regie houdt. Hoe je een beïnvloeder wordt van de weg naar het resultaat, van je omgeving, van je team én van je eigen effectiviteit

Languages: Nederlands
Available formats: Hard copy, eBook

Languages: Nederlands
Available formats:
Hard copy, eBook

Projectmanagement op basis van ICB versie 4 – 3de geheel herziene druk – IPMA B, IPMA C, IPMA-D , IPMA PMO

ISBN 978 94 018 0064 8

- Dit handboek 'Projectmanagement op basis van ICB versie 4' vervangt het zo succesvolle handboek 'Projectmanagement op basis van NCB versie 3'
- De inhoud is gebaseerd op de Individual Competence Baseline version 4 (ICB4) van de International Project Management Association (IPMA)

Languages: Nederlands
Available formats: Hard copy, eBook

Projectmanagement voor het HBO op basis van IPMA-D – Theorieboek

ISBN 978 90 8753 497 4

- Voor iedereen die zich wil opleiden voor projectmanagement
- Bestaat uit een theorieboek, bijbehorend werkboek en een website
- Opzet van het theorieboek is in de volgorde waarin een project wordt aangepakt

Languages: Nederlands
Available formats: Hard copy, eBook

Projectmanagement voor het HBO op basis van IPMA-D – Werkboek

ISBN 978 90 8753 498 1

Dit Werkboek sluit aan op de inhoud van Projectmanagement voor het HBO op basis van IPMA-D – Theorieboek en de bij dit boek ontwikkelde website:
www.projectmanagementvoorhethbo.nl

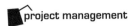

Languages: English
Available formats:
Hard copy, eBook

Better Practices of Project Management Based on IPMA competences – 4th revised edition
ISBN 978 94 018 0046 4

- This is the revised edition of the first text book in English specially developed for training for IPMA-D and IPMA-C exams, now based on Version 4 of the ICB
- In this 4th edition, the text has been restructured and extended to align with the structure and scope of the competence elements in the ICB version 4, divided into Practice competences, People competences and Perspective competences

Languages: Nederlands
Available formats: Hard copy, eBook

De kleine prinses – maakt projectmanagement stoer
ISBN 978 90 8753 675 6

- Dit sprookje verleidt de lezer op een plezierige wijze tot nadenken, het inspireert om anders te kijken naar zaken die vanzelfsprekend lijken

Languages: Nederlands
Available formats: Hard copy, eBook

De kleine prinses en de chaos in het project
ISBN 978 94 018 0011 2

- Dit moderne sprookje biedt waardevolle inzichten op het gebied van de chaostheorie en chaordische projecten, Rijnlands versus Angelsaksisch, werken op basis van vertrouwen en nog meer
- Het laat zien hoe je een project kunt leiden door het los te laten, in plaats van meer te structureren

PRINCE2® in de Praktijk –
Management Guide -
7 valkuilen, 100 tips
ISBN 978 90 8753 305 2

- Praktische toepassing van PRINCE2 Editie 2009
- Door de focus op 7 valkuilen en 100 tips wordt de methode hanteerbaarder
- Een must-have voor alle professionals die betrokken zijn bij PRINCE2-projecten

Languages: Nederlands
Available formats: Hard copy, eBook, ePub

Het Project Management Office – PMO
– Management Guide
ISBN 978 90 8753 134 8

- Bij projectmanagement moet ook de (lijn-) organisatie meegroeien
- Hoe zou een PMO binnen een organisatie er uit moeten zien?

Languages: Nederlands
Available formats: Hard copy, eBook

Project Management Office
implementeren op basis van P30®
ISBN 978 90 8753 546 9

- Voor iedereen die betrokken is bij de opzet of inrichting van een PMO
- Biedt handvatten voor het effectief besturen en inrichten van een veranderorganisatie
- Uitleg op welke wijze P30 organisaties ondersteuning kan bieden

Languages: Nederlands
Available formats: Hard copy, eBook

Languages: Nederlands
Available formats: Hard
copy, eBook

Managen van agile projecten - 2de herziene druk
ISBN 978 94 018 0024 2

- Dit boek beschrijft op eenduidige wijze
  de principes, processen, rollen en
  verantwoordelijkheden van de belangrijkste
  producten en technieken bij het managen van
  agile projecten. Daarbij wordt ook ingegaan op
  de verschillen en overeenkomsten met andere
  methoden zoals PRINCE2, Scrum Kanban en
  Lean Six Sigma en in hoeverre deze aanpak
  hiermee is te combineren

Languages: English, Dutch
Available formats:
Hard copy, eBook

Competence profiles, Certification levels and Functions in the project management field – Based on ICB Version 3 – 2nd revised edition
ISBN 978 90 8753 683 1

- Reference model for the development of
  function profiles for project managers and
  PMO's
- Complete function building for the project
  management field
- This official publication is endorsed by IPMA NL
  chapter

Languages: Nederlands
Available formats:
Hard copy, eBook

Scaling agile in organisaties
ISBN 978 94 018 0164 5

- Dit boek gaat over organisaties die stappen
  willen zetten om teams meer autonomie te
  geven door besluitvorming decentraal neer te
  leggen in managementlagen en managers weg
  te halen om de teams zelf-organiserend te laten
  optreden.

Het Project Management Office als serviceafdeling
ISBN 978 90 8753 727 2

- Dit boek biedt een nieuwe zienswijze op het inrichten van een Project Management Office
- Het boek maakt duidelijk dat professionele projectondersteuning een wezenlijke bijdrage levert aan het voortbestaan van de organisatie en dat projectmanagementondersteuning een absolute voorwaarde is voor succes
- Het boek gaat in op het '2 werelden'-fenomeen: de lijn- en de projectorganisatie

Languages: Nederlands
Available formats:
Hard copy, eBook

Duurzaam Projectmanagement
ISBN 978 90 8753 751 7

- Dit boek gaat over duurzaamheid in het managen van projecten
- In dit boeken geven de auteurs 'handen en voeten' aan duurzaam projectmanagement
- In het boek concrete toepassingen in de projectmanagementprocessen op basis van de methode PRINCE2

Languages: Nederlands
Available formats: Hard copy, eBook

Risicomanagement op basis van M_o_R® en NEN/ISO 31000
ISBN 978 90 8753 656 5

- Een brede inleiding over de internationale ontwikkelingen m.b.t. risicomanagement
- Nederlandse standaarden: COSO, NEN / ISO 31000:2009 en M_o_R
- Ook ter voorbereiding op het M_o_R Foundation examen

Languages: Nederlands
Available formats: Hard copy, eBook

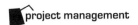

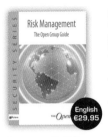

Risk Management: The Open Group Guide
ISBN 978 90 8753 663 3

- Supports many approaches: COSO, ITIL, ISO/IEC 27002, COBIT, OCTAVE and more
- Covers Taxonomy, Risk Assessment and Application of the FAIR approach
- Refers to Information Security: a pivotal issue in today's market

Languages: English
Available formats: Hard copy, eBook

ISO 21500 in Practice – A Management Guide
ISBN 978 90 8753 748 7

- This book explains the background, the value, the implementation and the application of ISO 21500 for each type of organization
- The book supplies answers to the 100 most common asked questions about ISO 21500 with the focus on the value of the guideline for the project management practice

Languages: English
Available formats: Hard copy, eBook

ISO 21500 Guidance on project management – A Pocket Guide
ISBN 978 90 8753 809 5

- This pocket guide provides a quick introduction as well as a structured overview of the ISO 21500, which also applies to national standards based on this standards (e.g. BSI, DIN, NEN, etc.)
- All ISO 21500 management themes are covered: Integration, Stakeholder, Resource, Scope, Time, Cost, Risk, Quality, Procurement and Communication

Languages: English
Available formats:
Hard copy, eBook, ePub

Languages: English
Available formats: Hard
copy, eBook, ePub

TOGAF® Version 9.1

TOGAF® Series

ISBN 978 90 8753 679 4

- The Official Hard copy publication of TOGAF, The Open Group Architecture Framework
- TOGAF is an open industry standard of enterprise architecture
- What is an architecture framework? What kind of 'architecture' are we talking about?
- How does my organization benefit from using TOGAF?
- This book provides the answers!
- TOGAF 9 complements, and can be used in conjunction with, other frameworks that are more focused on specific aspects of architecture

Reader's comments:

'Nothing less than a breakthrough in the world of Enterprise and IT Architecture', Ron Tolido, CTO Capgemini on TOGAF 9

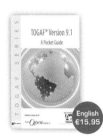

Languages: English, French, German, Dutch,
Brazilian Portuguese, Spanish (Latin American)
Available formats: Hard copy, eBook, ePub

TOGAF® Version 9.1 Enterprise Edition – A Pocket Guide

TOGAF® Series

ISBN 978 90 8753 678 7

- Pocket Guide on the TOGAF 9.1 framework
- Explains the main concepts of TOGAF Version 9.1
- Portable reference guide – and contains all the fundamentals

Languages: English
Available formats:
Hard copy, eBook, ePub

TOGAF® 9 Foundation Study Guide – 3rd Edition
Preparation for the TOGAF 9 Part 1 Examination

TOGAF® Series

ISBN 978 90 8753 741 8

- This is the Offical Open Group Study Guide
- Study Guide for Preparing for the TOGAF Part 1 Examination
- Contains Official sample questions
- Handy reference guide

Languages: English
Available formats:
Hard copy, eBook, ePub

TOGAF® 9 Certified Study Guide – 3rd Edition Preparation for the TOGAF 9 Part 2 Examination

TOGAF® Series

ISBN 978 90 8753 742 5

- Official sample exam
- A complete and thorough explanation of all key concepts
- Contains Exercises and Recommended Reading
- A Test Yourself examination paper is included
- Already more than 25,000 people are TOGAF Certified

Languages: English
Available formats:
Hard copy, eBook

The Open FAIR™ Body of Knowledge – A Pocket Guide

ISBN 978 94 018 0018 1

- This pocket guide provides a first introduction to the Open FAIR™ Body of Knowledge
- The Open FAIR Body of Knowledge provides a taxonomy and method for understanding, analyzing and measuring information risk
- The outcomes are more cost-effective information risk management, greater credibility for the information security profession, and a foundation from which to develop a scientific approach to information risk management

ArchiMate ® Certification Study Guide

The Open Group Series

ISBN 978 94 018 0002 0

- Published and supported by The Open Group
- Prepares for the ArchiMate 2 Part 1 and 2 Examinations
- The two Enterprise Architecture standards of The Open Group – TOGAF and ArchiMate – complement each other and can be used well in combination

Languages: English
Available formats: Hard copy, eBook, ePub

ArchiMate® 3.0 Specification
The Open Group Series

The Open Group Series

ISBN 978 94 018 0047 1

- ArchiMate® 3.0 is a major update to ArchiMate 2.1
- The two enterprise architecture standards of The Open Group complement each other
- Tool support for the ArchiMate language is already commercially available

Languages: English
Available formats: Hard copy, eBook

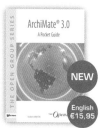

ArchiMate® 3.0 - A Pocket Guide

The Open Group Series

ISBN 978 94 018 0048 8

- This Pocket Guide is based on the ArchiMate® 3.0 Specification
- Published and supported by The Open Group; the independent, global organization
- ArchiMate is simple but comprehensive enough to provide a good structuring mechanism for architecture domains, layers and aspects
- ArchiMate incorporates modern ideas of the 'service orientation' paradigm

Languages: English
Available formats:
Hard copy, eBook

SOA Source Book

The Open Group Series

ISBN 978 90 8753 503 2

- The SOA Source Book will help enterprise architects to use SOA effectively
- What is SOA and how to evaluate SOA features in business terms
- Explains how to use The Open Group Architecture Framework (TOGAF) for SOA

English
€29,95

Languages: English
Available formats: Hard copy, eBook

Wegwijzer voor methoden bij enterprise-architectuur – 2de herziene druk

ISBN 978 90 8753 802 6

- Dit boek is ontwikkeld vanuit de afdeling Architectuur van het Ngi
- Ondersteuning bij het kiezen en gebruiken van elf enterprise-architectuurmethoden
- Bevat interviews met toonaangevende enterprise-architecten

Dutch
€39,95

Languages: Nederlands
Available formats: Hard copy, eBook

Bedrijfsarchitectuur op basis van Novius Architectuur Methode

ISBN 978 90 8753 738 8

- Een boek over bedrijfsarchitectuur bestemd voor managers én informatiemanagers
- Beschrijft werkzame oplossingen voor bedrijfsarchitectuur
- Gebaseerd op jarenlange ervaring van de auteurs en in uiteenlopende organisaties

Dutch
€44,95

Languages: Nederlands
Available formats: Hard copy, eBook

Languages: English
Available formats:
Hard copy, eBook

The IT4IT™ Reference Architecture, Version 2.1
ISBN 978 94 018 0112 6

- The official manual of the IT4IT™ Reference Architecture, Version 2.1, an Open Group Standard. This is a vendor-neutral, technology and industry-agnostic reference architecture for managing the business of IT
- It comprises a reference architecture and a value chain-based operating model. The IT Value Chain has four value streams supported by a reference architecture to drive efficiency and agility

Languages: English
Available formats:
Hard copy, eBook, ePub

IT4IT™ for Managing the Business of IT – A Management Guide
ISBN 978 94 018 0031 0

- This Management Guide provides guidance on how the IT4IT Reference Architecture can be used within an IT organization to manage the business of IT
- It is designed to provide a guide to business managers, CIOs, IT executives, IT professionals, and all individuals involved or interested in how to transition an IT organization to become a Lean and Agile IT service provider

Languages: English
Available formats:
Hard copy, eBook

The IT4IT™ Reference Architecture, Version 2.1 – A Pocket Guide
ISBN 978 94 018 0169 0

- This Pocket Guide provides a concise introduction to the IT4IT™ Reference Architecture, Version 2.1, an Open Group Standard
- This standard provides a vendor-neutral, technology-agnostic, and industry-agnostic reference architecture for managing the business of IT, enabling insight for continuous improvement
- This Pocket Guide is authoritative with material derived from the official IT4IT documentation and contributions from members of the IT4IT Forum

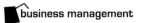

eSourcing Capability Models

(eSCM-Set)

ISBN 978 90 8753 606 0

- The ITSqc Series brings readers and users the ITSqc best practices
- Series includes the acclaimed eSCM models on e-sourcing
- Used worldwide by major IT sourcing firms, clients and advisors

Languages: English
Available formats: Hard copy

eSourcing Capability Model for Client Organizations

(eSCM-CL)

ISBN 978 90 8753 559 9

- Supports client organizations to successfully delegate IT-intensive business activities
- Practical details of the full range of client-organization tasks
- Guidance to complement existing quality models, standards and sourcing frameworks.

Languages: English, French
Available formats: Hard copy, eBook

eSourcing Capability Model for Service Providers

(eSCM-SP)

ISBN 978 90 8753 561 2

- Provides clients with an objective means of evaluating the capability of service providers
- Offers service providers a standard to differentiate themselves from competitors
- Designed to be used with other well-known standards and guidance

Languages: English
Available formats: Hard copy, eBook

Languages: nederlands
Available formats:
Hard copy, eBook

BiSL® - Een Framework voor business informatiemanagement - 2de herziene druk
ISBN 978 90 8753 687 9

- BiSL geeft invulling aan de processen en activiteiten die noodzakelijk zijn om de informatievoorziening vanuit de business, dat wil zeggen vanuit gebruikers- en bedrijfsoptiek te sturen
- In dit boek worden het BiSL-framework en de processen daarbinnen beschreven. Het biedt uitgebreide uitleg van alle aspecten en geeft handvatten om er zelf in de eigen organisatie mee aan de slag te gaan
- Dit boek is de tweede herziene druk van de officiële uitgave van ASL BiSL Foundation dat het Framework BiSL® beschrijft

Languages: English
Available formats:
Hard copy, eBook

BiSL® NEXT – A Framework for Business Information Management
ISBN 978 94 018 0039 6

- This book describes the framework of the next generation of Business Information Services Library, BiSL®
- BiSL Next is a public domain standard for business information management with guiding principles, good practices and practical templates
- This book offers guidance for digitally engaged business leaders and those who collaborate with them, with the ultimate goal to improve business performance through better use of information and technology.
- Twelve elements - four drivers, four domains and four perspectives - are the basis of the guidance in BiSL® Next

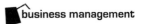

Languages: English
Available formats:
eBook, ePub

The BRMP® Guide to the BRM Body of Knowledge

ISBN 978 94 018 0022 8

- The BRMP® Guide to the BRM Body of Knowledge is designed to assist the Business Relationship Management Professional (BRMP®) training course attendees and certification exam candidates, but it will also be of great value to anyone looking for a comprehensive foundation-level overview of the art and practice of Business Relationship Management
- The book covers the entire BRMP® course syllabus and contains all the information covered in the training and referenced in the exam

Languages: English, Dutch
Available formats:
Hard copy, eBook

Business Transformation Framework – To get from Strategy to Execution

ISBN 978 94 018 0026 6

- This book explains the Business Transformation Framework, BTF Version 2016, a structural approach based on best practice
- It is a practical approach that helps organizations to design, develop, plan and govern organizational change
- Obviously developing a solid and widely supported Change plan is the first step towards a successful organizational change! The BTF approach imposes the establishing of coherence between organizational setting, strategy, and business transformation portfolio as well as between the four different aspects of running the business: Customer Treatment & Channels, Processes & organizational culture, Information & applications and IT infrastructure & facilities

Business Transformatie Framework - een raamwerk voor organisatie-verbetering

ISBN 978 94 018 0641 1

NEW

Dutch €39,95

Languages: Nederlands
Available formats: Hard copy, eBook

- Dit boek beschrijft het BTF, afkorting voor Business Transformatie Framework, een op best practice gebaseerde methodische aanpak voor Businesstransformatie

- Het is een praktische methode die organisaties helpt bij het ontwerpen, ontwikkelen, plannen en besturen van organisatieveranderingen Het maken van een goed en gedragen veranderplan is immers de eerste stap van een succesvolle verandering

- De methode dwingt tot het aanbrengen van samenhang tussen omgeving, strategie en veranderportfolio alsmede tussen de vier verschillende aspecten van de bedrijfsvoering: Klanten & dienstverlening, Processen & organisatie, Informatie & applicaties en ICTinfrastructuur & faciliteiten.

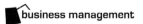

Cloud Computing for Business
ISBN 978 90 8753 657 2

- The book has been specifically designed for business managers
- Expertly highlights all the benefits that can be achieved via Cloud
- Official publication of The Open Group

Languages: English
Available formats: Hard copy, eBook

Outsourcing Professional Body of Knowledge – OPBOK Version 10
ISBN 978 94 018 0000 6

- Aligns with the IAOP Certified Outsourcing Professional® (COP) certification and training V10
- A complete Reference Guide for all Outsourcing professionals
- Practical guidance and checklists

Languages: English
Available formats: Hard copy, eBook

IT Outsourcing – An Introduction
ISBN 978 90 8753 492 9

- New, revised edition based on the best practices in IT Outsourcing
- Useful as a study guide for introduction courses in sourcing
- Endorsed by Platform Outsourcing Netherlands (PON)

Languages: English, Dutch
Available formats: Hard copy, eBook

IT Outsourcing Part 1:
Contracting the Partner
ISBN 978 90 8753 030 3

- A guide for Procurement Professionals asked to procure in this specialist area
- Ideal background for IT Managers who have to manage contracts
- Critical topic for all organizations focussing on core competences

Languages: English
Available formats: Hard copy, eBook

IT Outsourcing Part 2:
Managing the Sourcing Contract
ISBN 978 90 8753 616 9

- Expert guide to provide practical and concise advise on best practices
- Includes: contractmanagement, governance frameworks and relationshipmanagement
- a collaborative customer-driven business approach

Languages: English
Available formats: Hard copy, eBook

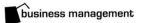

Languages: Nederlands
Available formats:
Hard copy, eBook

Het regiebureau – Kernprincipes voor sturen op resultaat
ISBN 978 94 018 0019 8

- Centraal in dit boek staan de kernprincipes van succesvol regie voeren op zakelijke dienstverlening bij organisaties middels de inrichting van een regiebureau
- De principes, methodes en uitgangspunten voor de inrichting van een regiebureau zijn zodanig beschreven dat ze bruikbaar zijn in verschillende disciplines van ondersteunende diensten en bij de primaire processen in iedere organisatie

Dutch
€29,95

Languages: English
Available formats: Hard copy, eBook

Implementing Strategic Sourcing
ISBN 978 90 8753 579 7

- Based on experiences in implementing and sustaining global sourcing
- Key guidance on the foundations, management, risk, governance and legal
- Successful principles for business development from a service provider perspective

English
€39,95

Languages: English
Available formats:
Hard copy, eBook

Operating Model Canvas
ISBN 978 94 018 0071 6

- The journey from strategy to operating success depends on creating an organization that can deliver the chosen strategy. This book, explaining the Operating Model Canvas, shows you how to do this
- The book contains more than 20 examples ranging from large multi- nationals to government departments to small charities and from an operating model for a business to an operating model for a department of five people
- The book contains two fully worked examples showing how the tools can be used to develop a new operating model

English
€39,95

NEW

Grip op Processen in Organisaties – 2de herziene druk
ISBN 978 90 8753 688 6

- Heldere toelichting van de stappen in een ontwerpproces, toegelicht met aansprekende voorbeelden
- Legt een relatie tussen het ontwerpen van een proces en de vervolgstappen bij de inrichting
- Behandelt de theoretische achtergrondkennis in hoofdlijnen

Languages: Nederlands
Available formats: Hard copy, eBook

Procesarchitectuur als veranderinstrument
ISBN 978 90 8753 550 6

- Behandelt de vijf hoofdstappen van de procesarchitectuur
- Complete integrale casus met vele praktische tips en zicht op de valkuilen
- Theoretische achtergrondkennis en een heldere blik op veranderende organisaties

Languages: Nederlands
Available formats: Hard copy, eBook

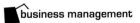

Contract and Commercial Management – The Operational Guide
IACCM Series
ISBN 978 90 8753 627 5

- A complete Reference Guide for all involved with Contract and Commercial management
- Also enriched with practical guidance and checklists
- Aligns with the official IACCM qualification and training

English
€59,95

Languages: English
Available formats: Hard copy, eBook, ePub

Fundamentals of Contract and Commercial Management
IACCM Series
ISBN 978 90 8753 712 8

- A complete introduction to basic principles for all involved with administration and day to day activities within Contract and Commercial management
- Practical guidance and checklists
- Aligns with the IACCM qualification and training

English
€34,95

Languages: English
Available formats: Hard copy, eBook, ePub

Handboek Managementmodellen
ISBN 978 90 8753 747 0

- Alle relevante managementmodellen in één boek
- Onmisbaar voor studenten HBO en WO en iedereen met een managementfunctie
- Het boek stimuleert ook om het eigen business-gevoel en intuïtie aan te spreken en niet te aarzelen om een meerzijdige diagnose te stellen

Dutch
€49,95

Languages: Nederlands
Available formats: Hard copy, eBook

CATS CM® editie 2014: Contractmanagement voor opdrachtgever en leverancier
ISBN 978 90 8753 721 0

- Dit boek is een inleiding tot contractmanagement voor bedrijven en overheid
- Geeft niet alleen een goede beschrijving van het nog jonge vakgebied contractmanagement, het levert ook een werkbare methode voor contractmanagers

Dutch €34,95

Languages: Nederlands
Available formats: Hard copy, eBook

Process Management Based on SqEME®
ISBN 978 90 8753 136 2

- Open standard for developing a process-centered architecture
- Innovativa and practical approach to precess-centered thinking
- For everyone involved in the change process in a process-driven organization

English €29,95

Languages: English
Available formats: Hard copy, eBook

SqEME® Process Management – A Pocket Guide
ISBN 978 90 8753 137 9

- Explains the theoretical and practical essentials on SqEME
- Contains practical essentials: supported by real-life case studies

English €15,95

Languages: English
Available formats: Hard copy, eBook

Van Haren Learning Solutions is an independent provider of learning solutions. Our focus is on making our content available in as many ways as possible, to as many people as possible.

Choose one of our methods and discover the possibilities!

 Best Practices & Study Guides. Best practices and methods in IT & IT Management, Enterprise Architecture, Business Management and Project Management.

 Courseware The ready-to-give course for trainer and student. Take a look at our portfolio.

 Exam training The extra preparation you need to pass the exam!

 eLearning The complete course online! Learn and study in any location and prepare yourself for the exam.

 Blended Learning The best of online and classical in one course! Combine the best of both methods.

 Gaming Play to learn! Test your knowledge and discover if you are ready for the exam.

What is Courseware ?

Courseware is 'high quality' accredited training material, available as softcopy or ebook publication. The Courseware includes a complete slide set and a variety of exercises, causes, practice exams, literature reference and the syllabus. Trainers can get the slide set by contacting sales@vanharen.net

What is a Courseware Package ?

A Courseware package is the above mentioned Courseware delivered together with the study book. The slides, exercises and the book are aligned completely and function supplementary to one and other. And provides a practical and supportive study experience. It also provides you with the best possible exam preparation.

Affiliated Only

By becoming an affilliated training organization of Van Haren Learning Solutions you can use the Courseware in order to obtain accreditation.

What is eDelivery ?

eDelivery are supplementary study products and delivery methods. This can be Online exam trainers, Online Pre-study material or eDelivery trainings that require a physical trainer. For our eDelivery portfolio, please visit: www.vanharen.net/academy

For more Info or our current portfolio, please visit: www.vanharen.net/learning-solutions

2 day training course

ITIL® Foundation Courseware - Package
ISBN 978 94 018 0081 5

The purpose of the course is to ensure that students gain an understanding of the IT Processes and then learn to manage IT services from their concept stage through design and development and safely into a production environment.

3 day training course

ITIL® Intermediate continual Service Improvement Courseware
ISBN 978 94 018 0141 6

All ITIL® Intermediate courses lead to individual ITIL® Certificates. These are free-standing qualifications, but are also part of the ITIL Intermediate Lifecycle stream, and are part of the modules that lead to the ITIL Expert Certificate in IT Service Management.

ITIL® Intermediate Service Strategy Courseware

3 day training course

ITIL® Intermediate Service Strategy Courseware

3 day training course

ISBN 978 94 018 0140 9

ISBN 978 94 018 0152 2

ITIL®
Intermediate
Service
Transition
Courseware

3 day training
course

ISBN 978 94 018 0137 9

ITIL®
Intermediate
Service
Operation
Courseware

3 day training
course

ISBN 978 94 018 0135 5

ITIL®
Intermediate
Release,
Control
and
Validation
Courseware

4 day training
course

ISBN 978 94 018 0145 4

ITIL® Service
Offerings and
Agreements
Courseware

4 day training
course

ISBN 978 94 018 0157 7

ITIL®
Intermediate
Operational
Support and
Analysis
Courseware

4 day training
course

ISBN 978 94 018 0148 5

ITIL®
Intermediate
Planning,
Protection
and
Optimization

3 day training
course

ISBN 978 94 018 0144 7

5 day training course

ITIL® Managing Across the Lifecycle
ISBN 978 94 018 0153 9

This 5 day training course leads to the
certification as ITIL®. Expert in ITIL®.

2 day training course

ITIL® Practitioner Courseware
ISBN 978 94 018 0156 0

This ITIL Practitioner qualification takes an entirely
new approach to service management education
and training.

2 day training course

TRIM (The Rational IT Model™)
Foundation Courseware - Package
ISBN: 978 94 018 0202 4

The Courseware package consist out of two
publications, TRIM (The Rational IT Model™)
Foundation Courseware
(ISBN: 978 94 018 0201 7) and TRIM:
The Rational IT Model
(ISBN: 978 94 018 0052 5).

This training consists of two days, which provide
preparation for the TRIM Foundation exam.

English
€ 96,25

2 day training course

Information Security Foundation based on ISO/IEC 27002 Courseware - Package
ISBN 978 94 018 0070 9

The Courseware package consist out of two publications, Information Security Foundation based on ISO/IEC 27002 Courseware (ISBN: 978 94 018 0060 0) and Foundations of Information Security Based on ISO27001 and ISO27002 3rd revised edition (ISBN: 978 94 018 0012 9).

English
€ 96,25

2 day training course

Information Security Foundation op basis van ISO 27002 Courseware Pakket
ISBN: 978 94 018 0178 2

Dit Courseware pakket bestaat uit twee publicaties: Information Security Foundation op basis van ISO 27002 Courseware (ISBN: 978 94 018 0179 9) en Basiskennis informatiebeveiliging op basis van ISO27001 en ISO27002 - 2de herziene druk (ISBN: 978 94 018 0013 6).

English
€ 96,25

COBIT® 5.0 Foundation Courseware Package
ISBN 978 94 018 0082 2

This three-day instructor-led, classroom-based course, provides an end-to-end business view of COBIT 5 – an internationally accepted framework for governing and managing enterprise IT that supports executives and management in their definition and achievement of business goals and related IT goals.

English
€ 96,25

2 day training course

Service Integration And Management (SIAM) Foundation Courseware Package
ISBN: 978 94 018 0219 2

The Courseware package consist out of two publications Service Integration And Management (SIAM) Foundation Courseware (ISBN: 978 94 018 0218 5) and Service Integration and Management Foundation Body of Knowledge (SIAM® Foundation BoK) (ISBN: 978 94 018 0102 7).

English
€ 96,25

2 day training course

Service Automation Framework Foundation Courseware - Package
ISBN: 978 94 018 0207 9

The Courseware package consist out of two publications, Service Automation Foundation Courseware (ISBN: 978 94 018 0205 5) and Service Automation Framework (ISBN: 978 94 018 0062 4).
Service Automation is the concept of achieving customer loyalty by the use of automated technologies and builds upon a large demographic and sociological trend. We are the self-service generation, who are able to make our own decisions. The self-service generation is nowadays used to searching, evaluating and purchasing products online.

English
€ 96,25

2 day training course

ASL® Foundation Courseware Pakket
ISBN 978 94 0180 159 1

Dit Courseware pakket bestaat uit twee publicaties, ASL® 2 Foundation Courseware en ASL® 2 - Een framework voor applicatiemanagement (ISBN: 978 90 8753 312 0).

De ASL 2 Foundation workshop is een training van 2 dagen die de deelnemers voorbereidt op het ASL 2 Foundation examen.

4 day traning course

IPMA-D op basis van ICB 4 Courseware Pakket
ISBN 978 94 018 0099 0

Dit cursuspakket bestaat uit twee publicaties, IPMA-D op basis van ICB 4 Courseware en het boek Projectmanagement op basis van ICB versie 4 – 3de geheel herziene druk – IPMA B, IPMA C, IPMA-D , IPMA PMO (ISBN: 978 94 018 0064 8).
De inhoud is gebaseerd op de Individual Competence Baseline version 4 (ICB4) van de International Project Management Association (IPMA).

4 day training course

IPMA-C op basis van ICB 4 Courseware Pakket
ISBN 978 94 018 0100 3

Dit cursuspakket bestaat uit twee publicaties, IPMA-C op basis van ICB 4 Courseware en het boek Projectmanagement op basis van ICB versie 4 – 3de geheel herziene druk – IPMA B, IPMA C, IPMA-D , IPMA PMO (ISBN: 978 94 018 0064 8).

Voor projectmanagers met minimaal 3 jaar ervaring op het gebied van projectmanagement.

4 day training course

IPMA-D based on ICB 4 Courseware Package
ISBN 978 94 018 0166 9

The Courseware package consist of two publications, IPMA-D based on ICB 4 Courseware and Better Practices of Project Management Based on IPMA competences – 4th revised edition (ISBN: 978 94 018 0046 4).

This training consists of four days, which provide preparation for the D exams. The course covers the subjects at a fast pace.

English
€ 172,50

5 day training course

IPMA-C based on ICB 4 Courseware Package
ISBN 978 94 018 0185 0

The Courseware package consist of two publications, IPMA-C based on ICB 4 Courseware (ISBN: 978 94 018 0184 3) and Better Practices of Project Management Based on IPMA competences – 4th revised edition (ISBN: 978 94 018 0046 4).
Certification is an important step in your professional development. IPMA-C is generally for project managers with a minimum of 3 years' experience.

Dutch
€ 96,25

2 day training course

PRINCE® Editie 2017 Foundation Courseware Pakket
ISBN 978 94 018 0049 5

Dit Courseware pakket bestaat uit twee publicaties, PRINCE2® Editie 2017 Foundation Courseware (ISBN: 978 94 018 0049 5) en Projectmanagement op basis van PRINCE2® Editie 2009 (ISBN: 978 94 018 0004 4).
Het Courseware is Nederlands en er wordt Engelse terminologie gebruikt, geschikt voor het Engelse PRINCE2® Editie 2017 examen. Tevens zijn er twee Nederlandse oefen examens van PRINCE2® 2009 toegevoegd voor studenten die toch liever het 2009 examen willen maken.

Dutch
€ 96,25

M_o_R® Courseware ter voorbereiding op het Foundation en practitioner Examen - Pakket
ISBN 978 94 018 0108 9

Deze Courseware bestaat uit twee samengevoegde publicaties, M_o_R® Courseware ter voorbereiding op het Foundation en Practitioner examen en Risicomanagement op basis van M_o_R® en NEN/ISO 31000 (ISBN: 978 90 8753 656 5). Het M_o_R® Courseware is te gebruiken bij de voorbereiding op het Foundation en Practitioner examen.

TOGAF® Foundation (Level 1) Courseware

ISBN 978 94 018 0172 0

The TOGAF® Foundation (Level 1) Courseware (ISBN: 978 94 018 0172 0) is based on TOGAF Version 9.1. TOGAF is a framework - a detailed method and a set of supporting tools - for developing an enterprise architecture, developed by members of The Open Group Architecture Forum.

TOGAF® Certified (Level 2) Courseware

ISBN 978 94 018 0173 7

The TOGAF® Certified (Level 2) Courseware (ISBN: 978 94 018 0173 7) is based on TOGAF Version 9.1. TOGAF is a framework - a detailed method and a set of supporting tools - for developing an enterprise architecture, developed by members of The Open Group Architecture Forum.

TOGAF® Foundation And Certified (Level 1 & 2) Courseware
ISBN 978 94 018 0174 4

The TOGAF® Foundation and Certified
(Level 1 & 2) Courseware
(ISBN: 978 94 018 0174 4) is based on
TOGAF Version 9.1. TOGAF is a framework
- a detailed method and a set of supporting
tools - for developing an enterprise architecture,
developed by members of The Open Group
Architecture Forum.

TOGAF brings business-, information- and
infrastructure architecture together. It is the
process for doing Enterprise architecture.
During these four or five day courses you will
become familiar with all aspects of TOGAF 9 and
Enterprise Architecture.

ArchiMate® 3.0 Foundation and Practitioner (Level 1 & 2) Courseware
ISBN 978 94 018 0217 8

This courseware is based on ArchiMate 3.0. The
ArchiMate Specification is a modelling language
that enables Enterprise Architects to describe,
analyze and visualize relationships among
architecture domains using easy to understand
visuals representations.

A training in ArchiMate will give you knowledge
about theoretical and practical aspects of
ArchiMate and is useful if you wish to be able to
apply this modelling language in practice.

2 day training course

BiSL® Foundation Courseware - Nederlands Pakket
ISBN 978 94 018 0051 8

BiSL staat voor business information services library en is hèt framework voor business informatiemanagement. Sinds de introductie van BiSL is het model uitgegroeid tot de standaard op het vakgebied in Nederland. BiSL biedt een structuur en leidraad voor business informatiemanagement. BiSL legt verbindingen tussen operationeel functioneel beheer en strategisch informatiemanagement en geeft handvatten voor (verdere) professionalisering van business informatiemanagement.

3 day training course

BiSL® Advanced Courseware
ISBN 978 94 018 0068 6

Deze Courseware bestaat uit twee samengevoegde publicaties, BiSL® Advanced Courseware en Aanvullende literatuur BiSL® Advanced examen (ISBN: 978 94 018 0066 2).

BiSL Advanced gaat in op "hoe" zou je het kunnen doen: hoe kun je business informatiemanagement inrichten, welke rollen kun je onderscheiden, welke hulpmiddelen zijn er in de business.

2 day training course

BiSL® Foundation Courseware - English Package
ISBN 978 94 018 0190 4

The Courseware package consist out of two publications, BiSL® Foundation courseware - English (ISBN: 978 94 018 0189 8) and BiSL® - A Framework for Business Information Management - 2nd edition (ISBN: 978 90 8753 702 9).